"Do What I Say"

✦ ✦ ✦

MS. BEHAVIOR'S
GUIDE TO
GAY & LESBIAN
ETIQUETTE

"Do What I Say"

MS. BEHAVIOR'S GUIDE TO GAY & LESBIAN ETIQUETTE

✦ ✦ ✦

By Meryl Cohn

HOUGHTON MIFFLIN COMPANY
BOSTON • NEW YORK
1995

For information about permission to reproduce selections
from this book, write to Permissions, Houghton Mifflin Company,
215 Park Avenue South, New York, New York 10003.

For information about this and other Houghton Mifflin trade
and reference books and multimedia products, visit
The Bookstore at Houghton Mifflin on the World Wide Web
at http://www.hmco.com/trade/.

Library of Congress Cataloging-in-Publication Data
Cohn, Meryl.
"Do what I say" : Ms. Behavior's Guide to gay & lesbian
etiquette / Meryl Cohn.
p.   cm.
ISBN 0-395-74538-1
1. Gay men — United States — Social conditions. 2. Gay men
— United States — Sexual behavior. 3. Etiquette for men —
United States. 4. Gay male couples — United States — Social
conditions. 5. Lesbians — United States — Social conditions.
6. Lesbians — United States — Sexual behavior. 7. Etiquette
for women — United States. 8. Lesbian couples — United
States — Social conditions. 9. Dating (Social customs) —
United States.   I. Title.
HQ72.2.U5C65   1995   95-9321
646.7'008'664 — dc20   CIP

Printed in the United States of America

QUM 10 9 8 7 6 5 4 3 2 1

FOR SARAH ALONSO
AND IN MEMORY OF STEVE KALMAN

ACKNOWLEDGMENTS

✦ ✦ ✦

My gratitude goes to the following people, who have offered their wisdom, opinions, comedic intervention, and friendship, and/or allowed me to write about their personal lives without too much of a fuss: Figs Mackenzie, Blanche McCrary Boyd, Wendy Liebman, Kevin Redmond, Stephanie Hodal, Philip Deschamps, the late Tom Sartini, Douglas Truesdale, Doug Cohn, Tom McWilliams, Steve Delfosse, Ken Golluscio, Joann Post, Jo Gabriel, Rich Van Loan, Jon Gothing, the Lesbians, Lynda Finn, and Jim Stroh. (I am hoping that whoever I may have forgotten will soon master the beautiful art of forgiveness.)

Many thanks to Gene London Collection NYC, Echo Scarfs, Kenneth Cole, Kenneth Jay Lane, and Mister Vito for lending props for the illustrations in this book, and to Faith Meade, stylist; Kate Best, makeup; Benno Friedman, photography; and Charles Kreloff, art direction.

My appreciation goes to Boston's *Bay Windows,* where Ms. Behavior's column was originally (and still is) published, particularly to Rudy Kikel, arts editor; to Dawn Seferian, my editor at Houghton Mifflin; and to the late Diane Cleaver, my agent.

I would like to offer special thanks to Sarah Alonso, who has consistently and generously offered her ideas, insight, editorial help, and always wonderful wit and humor.

CONTENTS

✦ ✦ ✦

Part Three

✦ ✦ ✦

GAY & LESBIAN CULTURAL ODDITIES THAT MS. BEHAVIOR FINDS PARTICULARLY COMPELLING

Part Four

✦ ✦ ✦

GAY MEN & LESBIANS IN A STRAIGHT ENVIRONMENT

Part Five

✦ ✦ ✦

SEX & DATING

Part Six

✦ ✦ ✦

FALLING IN LOVE & STAYING IN LOVE

CONTENTS

INTRODUCTION

✦ ✦ ✦

Ms. Behavior has written this book because she has always wished it existed. She especially longed for a book like this when she was a preteen dyke-in-training, unable to reconcile her attraction to comfortable shoes with her mother's need to buy her feminine, fashionable footwear.

If only Ms. Behavior had had some guidance, coming out might have been easier. She might have gone on fewer dates with scary people. Perhaps she wouldn't have had her first steamy lesbian experience on a weekend when her parents were visiting her at school. And it might even have been unnecessary for Ms. Behavior to spend endless nights crying herself to sleep, clutching her toy fire engine to her breast.

Where do you turn for advice if you're a gay man or lesbian? Although your very supportive therapist insists that she isn't grossed out by your sex life, she still doesn't get all the queer little everyday subtleties that concern you. Your mother can't help you, because she's just learning not to retch when you say the word "lover." And there are some questions that are just too embarrassing to ask your friends.

Not knowing how to behave in any social situation can cause a lot of angst and give you a headache, so Ms. Behavior aims to relieve some of the uncertainty in dealing with circumstances in your ordinary life. She hopes, in fact, to help you to achieve a state of enlightened, meditative bliss.

In investigating each of the topics in this book, Ms. Behavior sometimes acts as adviser, sometimes observer, and sometimes adventurer. She likes to think of herself as an astronaut exploring gay and lesbian life, even if in a particular chapter she happens to be exploring only her own cervix.

For a long time now, gay men have remembered to laugh at the idiosyncrasies and campy pleasures of gay culture; even lesbians (who have occasionally been accused of humorlessness) are beginning to learn to chuckle. Ms. Behavior feels that despite the battles that remain, gay and lesbian culture has evolved to a point where we can afford to enjoy some laughter directed at our own irresistible quirks and customs.

And what about straight people? Some heterosexuals crave a window through which they can understand gay and lesbian culture (or perhaps get a surreptitious glance at what they secretly think they might be missing). Although Ms. Behavior has written this book primarily for gay men and lesbians, she welcomes her enlightened straight readership to learn about size queens, wimmin's music festivals, dressing in drag, and lesbian vegetarian potluck dinners, as well as the ways in which gay men and lesbians are forced to confront conflicts about fitting in.

Ms. Behavior hopes you enjoy her book. Please let her know if there is anything else with which she can help. She is only too happy to provide you with the answers to all of your questions and solutions for all of your problems. She would like to be the salve for your pain and the balm you spread on your wounds.

In Love and Light,
Ms. Behavior

Part One

THE GIRLS:
LESBIAN RITUALS,
CULTURE, &
FASHION

Chapter One

✦ ✦ ✦

IS THIS JUST A PHASE, OR ARE YOU A REAL LESBIAN?

Okay, so you were your gym teacher's pet in high school and had a torrid fling with a babe named Muffy at your Seven Sisters college, but does that necessarily mean that you qualify as a Real Lesbian? Ms. Behavior thinks not. In these days of lesbian chic, the walls surrounding our flourishing community seem unusually permeable. Excited postadolescent women with flushed cheeks flow in and out of our collective warm embrace like so many slippery paramecia, reading Vita Sackville-West by day and *On Our Backs* when the sun goes down. They comfortably hold hands in the street and boldly touch tongues in the dimly lit corners of cafés. But now that being a Real Lesbian is oh so cool, lesbian behavior is not enough — you have to work harder than ever to earn your labrys necklace.

"Those feelings" may have started when you were four or when you were twenty. One day you touched another girl and a hot glow spread through your face and body. You were probably scared and delighted and felt like throwing up. This is normal.

3

Ms. Behavior was an eight-year-old at Camp Starlight when it happened to her. Her counselor, a voluptuous seventeen-year-old blonde named Fern, who was lying in bed wearing a nightgown, pulled the small, somewhat bucktoothed Ms. Behavior to her chest in a friendly embrace, and Ms. Behavior was overwhelmed with weird, delicious feelings. Fearful that someone might notice her reaction, she quickly threw herself to the floor and crawled away, pretending to have been shot. (Ms. Behavior has always been gifted in the fine art of subtlety.) Luckily, no one seemed to be looking, but for the rest of the day, during kickball, volleyball, and macaroni art, Ms. Behavior stood alone, distracted in her shorts and red Keds, quietly contemplating her burgeoning sensations.

Now, what about you? You do not have to get defensive about this sort of self-evaluation. (You can do it quietly, in the privacy of your own bedroom, with the help of a mirror.) Regardless of your conclusion, it is unlikely that anyone will try to confiscate your sapphic membership card. But Ms. Behavior must warn you that the strength of your conviction about being a lesbian, particularly if you have not yet lived much beyond adolescence, does little to predict whether or not you will remain in the fold.

When you came out to your mother, she probably tried to convince you that it was just a phase, even if you already had your crew-cut and tattooed first lover hanging from your arm. This is because mothers, who have perfected the everyday practice of Olympic denial, tend to think of your desire for relationships with women as an inconvenient problem, like impetigo, which will eventually pass. (Some also think that impetigo and lesbianism can both be caught from the sandbox.) This attitude, of course, only reinforces your certainty about your sexuality, so that you cannot (at least for the next four or five years) even contemplate the remote possibility that your dalliance with Madame Crew Cut is just that, a girl-girl fling. So you become committed to your lesbianism with an intensity bordering on religious fervor, and you find yourself carrying banners in parades and decorating your leather jacket with stickers that say things like "How Dare You Assume I'm Heterosexual" or "Girls Lick Girls Here." That will teach your mother.

Ms. Behavior doesn't mean to rush you, but eventually you *will* need to acknowledge whether your attraction to women really is just a fleeting whim brought on by a desire to be as cool as the rest of your lacrosse team or you are really a lifer. Lots of people will try to answer this question for you, although none of them (with the possible exception of Ms. Behavior) can really tell. If you express any doubt at all about your sexuality, your straight friends will try to convince you that you are straight but somehow damaged by love, and your lesbian friends will tell you that you are struggling with your own internalized homophobia and you should just get over it and accept yourself.

Ms. Behavior, however, would never tell you any of these things, because unlike your mother and your friends, she is perfectly loving and accepting and wants nothing more than your happiness. She will also acknowledge that there is a lot more overlap and back-and-forth than even most of us lifers seem to realize. When she attended her own Seven Sisters college tenth reunion recently, Ms. Behavior was somewhat appalled to discover how many of the leading lesbians of her day had climbed over the fence and were now proudly showing off their geeky Ivy League husbands. She was further crushed to find several formerly scary, speculum-wielding members of the Womyn's Resource Center now demurely carrying snapshots of their suburban homes and drippy-nosed children. The last straw, however, was when Buffy Bacon-Jones, the revolutionary dyke responsible for painting the school president's house lavender, showed up in lacy girl-drag with a bespectacled accountant-type male in tow and giggled at his every utterance. Ugh.

Are you getting nervous? Could this sort of June Cleaverish con-version actually happen to *you,* even though you feel safely ensconced in the loving arms of the lesbian community? Ms. Behavior hopes not. She does want to add, however, that although her heart breaks every time a fledgling lesbian undergoes that awkward transformation into straight-girlhood, she will support you and love you no matter what.

Ms. Behavior will now provide some questions you might ask yourself, which will help you to determine your authenticity as a Real Lesbian and perhaps even offer you some clues as to how to maintain your standing. (Remember when you score yourself that Real Lesbians are fair and honest.)

1. Have you been in a series of long-term monogomous relationships with women for which you have purchased matching silver rings?

2. Do you find that on some days, particularly if you are involved in a long, comfortable relationship, you like cuddling almost as much as you like sex?

3. Have you ever owned a copy of *Lavender Jane Loves Womyn?*

4. When you go to the beach, do you put your blanket down a mere six inches away from another lesbian, even if the entire beach is empty? (Hint: Real Lesbians have no boundaries.)

5. Do you use the word "process" as a verb in everyday conversation, even when not referring to film or meat?

6. Do you now or have you ever worn patchouli?

7. Do you have a strong sense of right and wrong about which you feel that no one had better cross you?

8. If you ever attempt to wear pantyhose, does most of it end up bunched up around your knees with the crotch hanging too low?

9. Can you stroll through the cosmetics section at Macy's without being tempted to buy anything?

10. Do you believe there is really no question about Whitney, Jodie, and Olivia?

11. Did you continue to leave your legs unshaven even after college ended?

12. Did you bemoan the demise of the Earth Shoe and then rejoice when the Birkenstock was invented?

13. Do you and/or your closest friends eat tempeh?

14. Is softball more than just a game to you?

15. Can you name all of Martina's ex-lovers?

Scoring: Give yourself one point for every yes.

Twelve to fifteen points: No matter what you ever wear or do, you are a big dyke to the core, and no one and nothing will ever take that away from you. When scientific advances make cloning a reality, the lesbian underground will try to convince you to donate some DNA. Rejoice. You are the Real Thing.

Seven to eleven points: You are on fairly firm footing most of the time but have to watch that secret and insidious appreciation you still have for frilly frocks and pumps. When you feel yourself slipping away from the warm fold, be sure to get a lezzie cultural infusion, or we may really lose you. (While Ms. Behavior generally does not advocate attendance at lesbian concerts, she might make an exception for you if you feel inspired by that sort of thing. Just don't make it a habit.)

Zero to six points: Aw, g'wan. You're no lesbian. If the right man comes along tomorrow, you'll ride right off into the sunset. And in a couple of months, when your sex life with him turns dull, you'll be telling him that you're so open-minded you used to sleep with women once, a very long time ago.

Chapter Two

✦ ✦ ✦

FINDING YOUR NICHE WITHIN THE LESBIAN COMMUNITY

Sporting Dykes;
Earthy-Crunchy/Granola/Activist Dykes;
Lipstick Lesbians; Leather Dykes
with Green Hair, Multiple Piercings,
and Big Heavy Boots;
and I'm-Not-Really-a-Dyke Dykes

Early in your career as a lesbian, you realize that dyke culture is a lot like a giant high school; at Marianne Williamson lectures, dog shows, and Melissa Etheridge concerts, you notice several distinct clusters of lesbians, each consisting of women who are frighteningly similar in appearance and attitude. Soon you wonder, What's with all this sapphic clique stuff, and where do I fit in? Basically, this translates into deciding whether to remain a lonely outsider or plunge bravely into the depths of dyke conformity, as well as determining which bevy of babes to immerse yourself in.

During your search for identity, you will ask yourself serious, life-altering questions, like How do I deal with lesbians from other niches? Should I even bother trying to become a part of things, or should I just feign disinterest and hang out at home with my lover and eleven overfed cats?

Despite your thoughts to the contrary, you *do* need to become a part of things. And Ms. Behavior is happy to affirm that you will receive emotional sustenance from a group of women who are bound to become like family: weird, but somehow supportive. It's just a matter of deciding which warm, nurturant lesbian bosom(s) you want to rest your tired head against.

To those who are just coming out, Ms. Behavior offers these words of comfort: Do not despair, sweet lesbian. Ms. Behavior considers it her duty to help with your hard choices. She is your tireless guiding light, the warm, strong hand that will happily smooth the terrain for your journey of lesbian exploration. You do not need to thank her. Just be happy in your life, and that will be enough for Ms. Behavior.

The following description of each clique is designed to aid lesbian newcomers in determining where they fit in and to assist them in envisioning the life that lies ahead.

When you see a SPORTING DYKE, you will know what type she is. Sporting Dykes are easy to identify because they have that hearty, robust look that makes more sedentary lesbians (like Ms. Behavior) want to lie down. Even if a Sporting Dyke doesn't have an actual whistle hanging around her neck, you will come away from an encounter with her remembering it dangling there against her overdeveloped Adam's apple.

Sporting Dykes do not concern themselves with fashion. They always wear sweatpants or shorts, whether they are going to work, a job interview, or a party. (For really special or formal occasions, however, they don Mylar sweatsuits and an unsullied pair of sneakers.) These athletic lesbians cut their hair short and never use makeup, not even for their Olympic debuts. Skin care for Sporting Dykes consists merely of insect repellent.

Sporting Dykes share a special intimacy that other lesbians miss out on. It comes from constant exposure to each other's sweat, spit, and mucus. Ms. Behavior's friend Bonnie, a big Sporting Dyke whose current obsession is scuba diving, explains it like this: "We always get undressed in front of each other, which makes you feel kind of close. Plus, when you come up from a hundred feet under, sometimes you have some major snot dripping down your face, and one of your pals has to notice it and tell you to wipe it off. Few things make you feel more connected to another person."

If you are not a Sporting Dyke, it is important to remember never to consider going on an outing with one. Take heed of Ms. Behavior's warning, and you might not have to experience this potential scenario for yourself: A Sporting Dyke asks if you would like to go on a picnic. Since you assume you know what a picnic is, you say yes. You make yourself a sandwich and pack it in a zip-lock Baggie with a piece of fruit. The Sporting Dyke picks you up in her big black Bronco and takes you for a long ride through the wilderness. You feel safe and secure, because you are a trusting person and the Sporting Dyke has biceps the size of tree trunks.

After driving sixty or seventy miles, the Sporting Dyke parks in the center of what looks like a jungle. She pulls two canteens and a pair of extra hiking boots from her knapsack. Your eye twitches and you begin to sweat. But a quick look at her face confirms that it is too late; once the Sporting Dyke is out in the fresh air, she is like a dog that has smelled blood.

You hop out of the truck, feigning cheerfulness in an attempt to hide your horror, and ask where the picnic site is. She tells you it is "a little ways up the road." There is no road. Convinced that she is your leader and that you are the lone remaining member of some kind of psycho survivalist group, you allow the Sporting Dyke to take you on a trek through the woods. She refuses to stop even when your newly blistered ankles begin to bleed profusely. She has no sympathy. She is like a gym teacher on crack.

You realize that the only way you will ever get home is to feign injury. Now you throw yourself to the ground and twist your knee, unfortunately hurting yourself more than you had planned. The Sporting Dyke gingerly examines your mangled joint, then lifts you in her strong arms and carries you the whole way back to the Bronco like a powerful packhorse. Although you are delirious with fatigue and pain, the irony is not lost on you; she has risked your life and now she is saving you. But you are too happy about going home to remain angry, so in a weak moment of gratitude you acknowledge the very thing she needs to hear in order to be happy: you tell her she is your hero.

EARTHY-CRUNCHY/GRANOLA/ACTIVIST DYKES are the lesbians who make you feel that everything you do is wrong. No matter how many bottles and cans you leave out at the curb, they berate you for your aluminum foil usage. Your recycling efforts are merely an attempt to assuage your guilt. *Their* efforts, however, are evidence of their sincere commitment to serve the goddess that lives within.

Earthy-Crunchy/Granola/Activist Dykes wear colorful all-cotton clothing made by Guatemalan farmers who are paid fair wages by a lesbian-run importing collective. Their hair is unkempt, and they wear glasses whether or not they need them. They live in seventies-style *faux* socialist communes with a three-to-one ratio of cats to people. Their living quarters, decorated with Judy Chicago and Georgia O'Keeffe prints, are free of fragrances, men (including boy-children over the age of five), and refined sugar. Cris Williamson is still "filling up and spilling over" on their turntables, and they take turns cooking nonanimal, plant-based meals that are taste-free.

Earthy-Crunchy/Granola/Activist Dykes conduct house meetings several times a week to "process" their feelings. They carefully guard against saying anything "inappropriate" or allowing anyone else to; they would sooner poison themselves through red-meat consumption than utter anything racist, sexist, ageist, thinist, or abledist. They always have at least one "differently abled" womyn at the core of their group, whom they wheel around at various events and concerts. (Ms. Behavior has often suspected that if they can't find one, one of the more altruistic members of the group will break her own legs.)

Spending time with these wimmin is hardly a restful experience; you must be conscious of your every move and utterance. If, for example, a gaggle of Earthy-Crunchy/Granola/Activist Dykes sees you ignorantly drinking a cup of coffee produced by a company that mistreats its migrant workers, they will conduct a Shame-a-thon. This is an ancient sadistic lesbian ritual, which involves forcing you to sit in the center of a circle while each earnest dyke expresses intense concern for your values, reminding you that you are responsible for the downfall of Mother Earth and all of her children. Believe Ms. Behavior — it is far uglier than it sounds.

Since these wimmin are totally humor-free, a sense of humor will do no good in their presence. Nor can you resort to the old standby of talking about sex; they believe only in cuddling, stroking, and very specific clitoral stimulation. Anything else reminds them too much of penises, and they collectively vomit (primarily tofu and beans).

Earthy-Crunchy/Granola/Activist Dykes do not approve of Ms. Behavior. When Ms. Behavior becomes old and ready to retire, they will not let a troublemaker like her into one of their lesbian retirement homes. Oh well.

LIPSTICK LESBIANS are the dykes that straight men and teenage lesbians fantasize about. Attractive and usually successful, they are the women most likely to appear, in all their radiance, on the covers of mainstream magazines and as pinup girls for stories called "Why Lesbians Really Are Just Like Everyone Else." They flock in groups, like sorority sisters, to glamorous apartments in metropolitan areas after completing their studies at glamorous universities.

Lipstick Lesbians have nicely styled hair and carefully polished fingernails (so you won't guess where their fingers have been). But their high visibility stems from their careers and salaries; they work as editors, corporate managers, television anchorwomen, entrepreneurs, politicians, and actresses. Because of their lipstick and feminine accoutrements, they are not recognizable to the straight masses as lesbians, but the well-trained eye can pick up a couple of clues. For example, despite their overall assimilation into mainstream fashion, Lipstick Lesbians always sit comfortably, as if ready and able to operate heavy machinery at a moment's notice. And one whiff of their cologne reveals that it has probably been purchased in the men's department.

Lipstick Lesbians never play softball or attend wimmin's music festivals, and they frown upon socializing or dating out of their species. While not at all jockish, they maintain trim bodies by participating in aerobics classes and by lifting tiny weights with their personal trainers, who are careful never to encourage them to exercise enough to perspire or build unwanted muscle mass.

Ms. Behavior must warn you to be cautious if you're offered the opportunity to make love with a Lipstick Lesbian; ask her to wear mittens. Also, you will have to have a sense of humor about Whitney Houston wailing "I'm Every Woman" in the background.

LEATHER DYKES WITH GREEN HAIR, MULTIPLE PIERCINGS, AND BIG HEAVY BOOTS are the lesbians who terrify straight people. When they go out to shopping malls during the day, crowds of heterosexuals part like the Red Sea, pressing themselves against store windows to avoid inadvertently brushing against these scary-looking women.

Luckily, Leather Dykes with Green Hair, Multiple Piercings, and Big Heavy Boots mostly come out after dark, when you cannot see them very well. They have bad skin from living on greasy junk food and Coca-Cola, and they rarely brush their teeth. They listen to head-banger music, and whether or not they have any musical talent, they perform in all-girl bands, which are called things like the Red Hot Labias, and sing songs like "Fuck Me with Your Fingers."

Leather Dykes with Green Hair, Multiple Piercings, and Big Heavy Boots pierce each other's nipples, tongues, and clits without using any anesthetic. "Pain is part of the ritual," they tell you as they point the needle at you and ask if you would like to try it, sans ice.

Ms. Behavior wishes she could say more about Leather Dykes with Green Hair, Multiple Piercings, and Big Heavy Boots, but she cannot; she does not have any friends who fall into this category, because she is prone to feeling protective of her nipples and refuses to allow herself to be surrounded by people who make them feel unsafe.

As you might guess from their moniker, I'M-NOT-REALLY-A-DYKE DYKES do not consider themselves to be lesbians, despite the strange fact that they enter into very long sexual relationships with women and never sleep with men. The hallmark of an I'm-Not-Really-a-Dyke Dyke is that she will lie in bed next to her naked lover, her face still wet with love, and say, "I'm not really a lesbian, you know. I just love *you*." The funny part is that her dewy-eyed lover, overcome with ardor, will repeat the same sentence back to her, as if it is a line from a romantic love poem. Such words seem to have an aphrodisiac effect on these women, who will then resume passionate lovemaking, more excited than ever by the notion that neither of them is really lesbian.

I'm-Not-Really-a-Dyke Dykes work at conventional jobs, order their clothing from L. L. Bean catalogues, have middle-of-the-road taste in everything, and never, ever come out, not even to their inner children. Even their families think of these couples as spinster companions, and they are only too happy to maintain that image of themselves.

I'm-Not-Really-a-Dyke Dykes are appalled by Sporting Dykes, Earthy-Crunchy Dykes, Leather Dykes, and even Lipstick Lesbians; they feel that such women create a bad impression of lesbians everywhere, and that if they themselves were in fact lesbians, such other dykes would make them most uncomfortable.

Before you knock yourself out trying to decide which category you fall into, Ms. Behavior must now confess that you do not actually have a choice. As with your lesbianism, you were born into your classification, and that's where you belong. If you still can't tell where you fit in, despite Ms. Behavior's best efforts at illumination, take this chapter to your mother or your psychiatrist and ask.

Chapter Three

✦   ✦   ✦

HOW TO TELL IF YOU'RE BUTCH OR FEMME (OR, A BUTCH IS A BUTCH IS A BUTCH)

*M*s. Behavior is aware that by bringing up the butch/femme topic, she risks inciting the wrath of thousands of usually good-hearted lesbians, who may wish to trample Ms. Behavior's pulchritude with their cleats. But Ms. Behavior is committed to a life of living dangerously and saying what she thinks.

The iron fist of political correctness warns against acknowledging that the butch/femme phenomenon exists. But *you* know it does. So it is only when you are alone or surrounded by lesbians in the know that you feel safe to wonder, does it really mean anything if your lover does the laundry and makes dinner every night while you take out the garbage and install the phone jacks? Yes, Ms. Behavior thinks so. She thinks it means you're a Big Bad Butch.

The butch/femme issue can be difficult to swallow because it is frequently and erroneously framed, mostly by foolish heterosexuals, as a gender-identity issue. These misinformed dolts have no way of understanding lesbian sexuality other than as "Who's the man?" Don't waste your breath telling them that this is not a boy-girl thing, or that it is ignorant to construe the butch/femme business as imitative of designated male and female roles in straight culture. They will not get it.

Do not let it get to you, either. Ms Behavior knows some dykes who get so upset by the whole issue that they deny the very existence of the phenomenon, even as they pound nails into the wall to work out their rage about the matter, productively creating an extension on the house while their lovers sew lace curtains for the living room.

Butch and femme is not an either/or thing; it is a continuum, and can sometimes be rather subtle. There is a fluidity to the expression of either characteristic over time; you may be way more femme (or butch) now than you were three years ago, depending on what other changes have occurred in your life. You might have a fabulously delicate new lover, for example, who inspires you to new levels of butchitude; but once she leaves you for an ax-wielding Amazon, you might just go back to your regular medium-femme self. Additionally, Ms. Behavior finds that describing just how butch or femme someone really is sometimes can be accomplished only as a relative thing, as in "She's butcher than Jamie Lee Curtis but not as butch as Kate Clinton." That creates a pretty clear picture, doesn't it?

Although some women femme it up with clothing and accessories, Ms. Behavior likes to point out that true butchness or femmeness is really an internal thing. For example, no matter how high Jodie's hair is piled and no matter how low-cut or girly her gown might be on the night she receives her Oscar, she is still a tough butch babe to the core. (Let's also not discount the fact that she talks like a truck driver.) Geena Davis, in contrast, is an undisputed femme, and no amount of Thelmaesque rough talk or gun-wielding can disguise that fact. The point is that (a) you can never cover the true essence o' butch with makeup or clothing, and (b) a femme is a femme is a femme.

Butchness, however, is clearly not just a lesbian phenomenon; some straight women clearly have the B-gene without benefit of the means of expressing it in an L-relationship. Who, for example, is more butch than Katharine Hepburn? (Or even Jane Fonda, who Ms. Behavior suspects packs quite the metaphorical bulge beneath that aerobics leotard?) It's just that when straight women are butch, it is usually called something else.

Some of Ms. Behavior's lesbian readers have written to her claiming not to know where they fall on the butch/femme continuum, which Ms. Behavior finds quite odd. At the risk of sounding like their mothers, to these lesbians Ms. Behavior would have to say, "What's wrong with you? Haven't you been paying attention? Go look and see what's hanging in your closet." While clothing, as previously mentioned, cannot be used to determine the truth about who you are, it is at least an indication of where your aspirations lie.

Other lesbians are confused in another way, believing that they are femme when they're really butch, or vice versa. Ms. Behavior once heard the comedian Lea Delaria, in a serious moment, describe herself as femme. Ms. Behavior momentarily choked on her rice cake, and then went on with her life. After all, part of living a serene existence means realizing that there are some mistakes too large ever to attempt to correct.

Self-knowledge is a beautiful thing, however, and needs to be cultivated in all lesbians. Once you know yourself, you can function much more confidently in relation to other dykes, allowing them to spin frantically around your calm and reassuring center. This will make you feel hip and Zenlike. So here's an exercise in self-assessment for those of you who claim to be confused.

Do you wear your keys on a clip and hook them to your belt loop? If so, there's no question about the extent of your butchness.

This is much more an attitude thing than a clothing thing; just ask your mother. She probably still yells at you for wearing men's shoes, unless she has thoroughly given up on you.

If you're in that ambiguous slacks-and-blazer group, try this: Do you own a pair of women's shoes with even the teensiest heel? Do you have to borrow pantyhose if the occasion arises to wear them? And would you be able to don them unaided?

Are you attracted to low-slung, phallically influenced vehicles? That screams of butchness. Would you rather *be* Martina Navratilova than sleep with her? Butch again.

Okay. Now, the femme diagnosis involves visualization. Picture yourself on a camping trip. Does the very idea of sleeping in the woods make you feel nauseated? Do you immediately worry about whether you'd be able to take a shower and style your hair? If a spider crawled into your sleeping bag, would you make someone else kill it? If so, you've got the femme thing happening in a big way.

If you need further convincing, ask yourself these questions: Do you know when your clothing matches without having to ask anyone? Do you own more than three hair products, not including shampoo and conditioner? Would you rather look like Demi Moore than sleep with her? If you've answered yes to all of the above, you're a deep-down femme.

It has been Ms. Behavior's experience (or perhaps she should say observation) that a dyke's relative butchness or femmeness in daily living does not necessarily bear on how she behaves in the boudoir. You'll know what Ms. Behavior means if you've ever seen the button that says "Butch in the bar and femme in the car," which includes a line drawing of a big butch in the back seat, legs up in the air, squealing. So don't be confused by the frosted-hair, polished-nails, gold-chain "femme" who talks like a Marine sergeant in between spits, who you know would have you "yes, ma'aming" and saluting in bed. And that stone butch, ropy-muscled member of your softball team who smokes Lucky Strikes with an attitude Brando would have envied might go home at night only to be totally sexually dominated by her lipstick-wearing, lace-clad girlfriend, who ties her up and tickles her with feathers. (Of course, the so-called butch would rather die than tell you this.)

Butch lesbians in the know long ago discovered that some of their wildest evenings of pleasure can happen at the hands of a seemingly demure femme, who emerges between the sheets as a fierce orchestrator of love. The butch will resist at first; she always tries to defend against her own seduction, because she thinks she has to remain in control. In actuality, however, she longs to be rendered helpless so she can give up that tiring feeling of being in charge all the time. True butches are very exhausted people. If you are a femme who manages to maneuver a butch into that state, she is likely to be very grateful. She will envision you as her salvation. She will get down on her knees and beg you for more. She will fetch you things whenever you snap your fingers. It will be fun.

Chapter Four

✦ ✦ ✦

BEARDED WIMMIN:
NOT BY THE HAIR
ON YOUR
CHINNY-CHIN-CHIN

Ms. Behavior has received a slew of letters asking her opinion of bearded wimmin, those odd babes who hang together in cafés sipping herbal tea and thoughtfully stroking their fuzzy chins. While Ms. Behavior could not possibly begin to explain this phenomenon (primarily because she does not understand it herself), she does think that staring is very rude and should be discouraged. Besides, the consequences of gawking can cause facial disfigurement of a different kind.

It was when Ms. Behavior first started frequenting lesbian bookstores, way back in the twilight of her adolescence, that she became aware of this small and specialized society. Initially, there were just buttons proclaiming love for bearded wimmin, and then there were bumper stickers too. If "I Love Bearded Wimmin" wasn't enough, there was "Bearded Wimmin Turn Me On" and "Bearded Wimmin Keep a Stiff Upper Lip."

At first Ms. Behavior thought it might be a joke. It was not until she began attending lesbian concerts that she saw that bearded wimmin really did exist. Some flaunted long orange goatees and others sported dark, closely cropped beards. Even a few sparse wiry hairs constitute a beard for some women, who seem to care for and cultivate their prized hairs like flowers in a garden. (Ms. Behavior does not totally understand the connection between facial hair and lesbian concerts, but she guesses that in this subcategory of lesbian culture, a beard is like a badge of honor, in the same way that Sporting Dykes think muscles are to be nurtured like small pets and children.)

Bearded wimmin tend to travel in packs. Ms. Behavior speculates that this is simply because it is more comfortable to hang with others in the same fashion category, just as Lipstick Lesbians or Earthy-Crunchy/Granola/Activist Dykes seem to travel in groups. For those who are satisfied only by biological explanations of social phenomena, Ms. Behavior's other theory is that bearded wimmin are attracted by one another's pheromones.

For once, Ms. Behavior may have more questions than she has answers. Is this a butch thing? readers want to know. Probably. If a femme woman grew a few hairs on her chin, she would probably use some sort of depilatory. (For the record, so would Ms. Behavior.)

Is this a political thing? Probably. If it were not a means of expressing a *right* to grow hair, or an unwillingness to conform with society's standards, which require women to be hairlessly beautiful, they would probably just shave it off.

Do some women start out with maybe just a couple of baby-fine blond hairs sprouting on their chin and shave every day until it grows in thick and dark, like their mothers told them it would if they shaved the hair on their legs? The answer to this question is too scary to contemplate.

Should you grow a beard? Well, while you have every right to do so, Ms. Behavior strongly discourages it. Unless you're a man, and even then Ms. Behavior finds it queer.

Chapter Five

✦ ✦ ✦

WIMMIN'S MUSIC FESTIVALS: MS. BEHAVIOR'S NIGHTMARE

Ms. Behavior doesn't care if she is a bad lesbian; some lesbian rituals horrify her too much for etiquette to enter the picture. Do not, for example, invite Ms. Behavior to a wimmin's music festival. She can envision few things more frightening.

It's not that Ms. Behavior hasn't imagined what a wimmin's music festival would be like; she has nightmares about it all the time. Worse than her fear of feeling like an alien is the fear that she wouldn't feel like an alien. What if she were brainwashed and forced to assimilate into the strange culture?

At the start of Ms. Behavior's recurrent bad dream, she enters the campground and watches a bunch of hearty, tanned wimmin emerge from their trucks, toting tents and knapsacks on their muscular, tattooed shoulders. Once the tent pegs (or whatever you call them) are pounded firmly into the soft, rich earth, the wimmin begin to disrobe, shucking their jeans, their shirts, their underwear, everything but their hiking boots and tool belts (always the perfect place to carry an axe).

Ms. Behavior stubbornly keeps on her shorts, her T-shirt, and yes, even her bra, because she does not enjoy that free feeling some people associate with bouncing breasts, and also because she is white-skinned and prone to sunburn. Strapping Amazons stare at Ms. Behavior's clothing and cajole her to peel it off. Bearded wimmin stand around her in a naked circle, clapping and hooting, boobs bobbing in hypnotic rhythm. The sunlight bounces off the silver hoops piercing some wimmin's nipples, nearly blinding Ms. Behavior. Ms. Behavior closes her eyes and keeps her arms folded across her chest, refusing to undress. The lesbians whisper loudly about their sadness that some wimmin remain trapped by a culturally defined negative view of their bodies.

Determined not to be shamed into stripping, Ms. Behavior wanders around the campground alone. She inadvertently strays into the Scent-Free Zone, where she is accosted by wimmin with multiple chemical sensitivities, who do not allow deodorant or shampoo users to enter their territory. (The unwitting Ms. Behavior exudes the scent of Soft 'n' Dry from her armpits and Lori Davis products from her hair.) Two large-boned, naked wimmin, Becky and Noreen, forcibly drag Ms. Behavior to the river and scrub the offensive fragrances from her hair and skin while chanting, "Chemicals make us angry. Fragrances cause us pain."

After a long and vigorous scouring session, Becky and Noreen, now red-faced and exhausted, drop Ms. Behavior's limp body onto the riverbank. Becky, however, feels concerned that they may have hurt Ms. Behavior's feelings, so they carry her to the Hugging Tent. Here a bunch of large maternal lesbians insist on holding Ms. Behavior's face against their ample bosoms while stroking her hair and murmuring that it is "okay to need Mommy." Greta, the biggest, most maternal hugger, offers Ms. Behavior a large assortment of female stuffed animals. Tired and overwhelmed, Ms. Behavior is surprised to find herself clutching Daisy Duck.

The huggers keep Ms. Behavior for three hours, tickling her shoulders with peacock feathers and sprinkling her hair with patchouli. (She cannot enter the Scent-Free Zone again.) They whisper affirmations in her ears and encourage her to pound on the earth and cry, although gently, so she doesn't knock over the tent. The affirmations consist of such phrases as "Goddess, fill my body, Goddess, caress my breasts. I am a beautiful lesbian, with the strength to uproot trees and tents, but with the tenderness not to."

When Ms. Behavior decides she wants to leave, Greta first makes her eat homemade rice pudding, which is free of white sugar and dotted with raisins and dates. The huggers convince Ms. Behavior that it is a very comforting food, and despite her efforts to resist their persuasion, Ms. Behavior feels warm and sated. She is beginning to like it here.

Although she has been at the music festival for several hours, Ms. Behavior still has not heard any music. She does, however, hear the sound of various atonal lesbians chanting songs about developing compassion for trees, animals, and plants. "Ooooom. Aaaaaaaah." At first she remembers how much she dislikes that sort of thing, but as she walks toward the noise, she begins to lose her ability to judge it. It sounds kind of like music and kind of like praying or wailing, but whatever it is, it seems a little soothing, so Ms. Behavior heads in the direction of the sound, still clutching Daisy Duck.

On her way to the stage, or at least to where it seems the stage would be, Ms. Behavior stops by the Carrot Juice Tent for a drink. Behind the table, she sees a somehow familiar but naked blond womyn serving the juice. "Plain carrot, or carrot and green?" the blonde asks in a friendly way. The blonde is much smaller than she appears in the movies. Her thin lips are rimmed with green juice and her chest is streaked with carrot juice and dirt. Ms. Behavior tries not to look at her breasts.

Ms. Behavior asks for plain carrot, and the blonde serves it to her with a shy grin. "Don't be afraid — it will be safe," she whispers in her low, gravelly voice. "I only pretended to be an FBI agent. Can I invite you to the Massage Tent?"

Ms. Behavior is very tired and too weak to find her car or remember how to get to her hotel, so she agrees. She knows she is in the first stages of being brainwashed, but she can no longer sustain the effort to resist. Jodie entwines her fingers with Ms. Behavior's and they walk slowly together, stepping over a number of lesbians, now unified in various naked embraces, making sounds like whales.

The Massage Tent is dark and damp and filled with the smells of clashing incense. Wimmin are lying on tables and moaning while other, strong wimmin knead their muscles. Ms. Behavior decides that no matter what, she will not moan.

Jodie invites Ms. Behavior to climb onto a table. Ms. Behavior thinks about it for a moment, looking at Jodie's strong hands and imagining them stroking her body. She knows that a massage given by Jodie will make a good story to tell her friends, so she says, "Okay, but I'd like to keep my clothing on." Jodie laughs gently for a moment and then eases Ms. Behavior off the ground and tenderly lays her on the table. "I'm just taking off your shirt," she says, and Ms. Behavior lets her.

Ms. Behavior closes her eyes and sinks down into the massage table, waiting. She feels a pair of warm, strong hands on her shoulders, and another pair on her calves. Just as she begins to think she might like this after all, she opens her eyes for a second and . . . Jodie is gone. Like vapor. In Jodie's place are Becky and Noreen, who are massaging Ms. Behavior rather briskly.

Ms. Behavior gets frightened, but before she can cry out for help she sees her friend Greta from the Hugging Tent. When Becky and Noreen notice Greta approaching, they slip out through the side flap of the tent. Greta warmly hugs Ms. Behavior and strokes her hair, whispering reassuring slogans. Ms. Behavior makes a small sound, in spite of herself, and is so delirious that she thinks she might be happy.

She is too tired to leave or even to care about resisting the wimmin's music festival experience, so she just stands up, lets her clothing fall away, and takes a first naked stride toward the woods with Greta, who she has decided is a goddess.

Later that night, all the wimmin wait until the moon has reached its zenith and then dance to celebrate the summer solstice. Ms. Behavior is not sure whether it is the effect of incense inhalation, but the moon looks like a breast and all the wimmin's breasts look like moons, and the women dance together like rotations of the solar system, and Ms. Behavior realizes that she has come home.

Chapter Six

✦ ✦ ✦

WHY LESBIAN
THERAPISTS ARE
SCARY

*M*s. Behavior is humble enough to acknowledge that there may occasionally be times when the pressures of life are so overwhelming that you need more than her advice to pull you through. During such stressful periods, you may turn to the expertise of the great psychological establishment.

Ms. Behavior, who is an admirer of all lesbians, great and small, firmly believes in supporting lesbian-owned businesses and services. If you need your car fixed, Ms. Behavior will encourage you to take it to a lesbian mechanic; if you require a Pap smear, she will recommend a lesbian gynecologist. She draws the line, however, at unequivocal support for lesbian therapists, who she thinks are rather peculiar and sometimes downright frightening.

Ms. Behavior understands that when you are feeling distressed or sad about any area of your life, a lesbian therapist might seem like a good idea. After all, you are comfortable with lesbians, you can easily get a referral to one, and you won't have to worry about Dr. Good-

Dyke subtly trying to turn you straight. A sapphically inclined therapist might understand the intricacies of woman-to-woman love in a way that most heterosexual therapists could not, and you would feel comfortable filling her in on all the intimate and exciting details of your fabulous sex life without worrying that she would vomit on her Persian rug or her shiny black pumps. But there *are* other factors to consider.

First of all, lesbian therapists often commit unforgivable fashion violations, which can be very distressing as you sit there discussing the maudlin details of your childhood. Prone to wearing natural-fiber drawstring pants and big colorful ponchos, lesbian therapists have Partridge Family shag haircuts and wear thick orthopedic-style sandals. Truly authentic lesbian therapists don jewelry made only by their sisters, consisting of numerous crystals, labia-like earrings, and rings with double wimmin signs. Burning incense is a ritual during each session, as flute music with accompanying vocals about sisters cultivating the farmland plays softly in the background.

Lesbian therapists never have long or polished fingernails; their nails are frequently bitten down to the bloody quick, revealing more about their own neuroses (and perhaps their sexual habits) than you want to know. Now, here's what Ms. Behavior urges you to consider: Do you need to be exposed to all of these disturbing stimuli during your time of distress? Won't these distractions interfere with your healing process? Instead of focusing on getting the help you need, you will be busy asking her to sit on her hands during the session, or making arrangements to pay with Lee press-ons or Isotoner gloves.

Lesbian therapists are six times more likely than straight ones to insist that you need to experience things like primal scream therapy and rebirthing. They are fluent in therapyspeak and goddess language and prone to saying things like "When you release your tears, do you feel yourself to be at one with Mother Earth and the rain forest?" or "How does the Goddess Within feel about seeing her family tonight?"

Ms. Behavior must further warn you that if you remain in therapy with a lesbian therapist, you will surely be forced to pummel a pillow with a bat while she beats a drum and chants a song about strong and beautiful Amazons. Worse yet, if you actually allow yourself to let go and get into the rage and pounding, your lesbian therapist will ask you to put a sound to it.

Most problems with lesbian therapists, however, stem from a lack of boundaries. Poor Boundary Disorder is easy to diagnose: Your lesbian therapist has PBD if she says and does intrusive things that make you want to bolt. Conducting therapy sessions in her cozy kitchen or "sharing" her feelings about her lover's big new Harley would be minor infractions on the boundary-violation continuum; taking you home for a millet dinner and offering you a back rub with musk oil to release your psychic tension would be major. (And as tempted as you might be, Ms. Behavior advises you to refuse her offer firmly.)

Most boundary violations are subtler than this; some are even quite unintentional. For example, what do you do when you run into your lesbian therapist in Provincetown? This happened to Ms. Behavior several years ago, back when she had a dyke shrink. Ms. Behavior was walking peacefully on the beach when she suddenly saw her lesbian therapist, Dr. Rachel Rabinowitz-Glick, PBD, lying topless on a towel next to her chubby lover, her nipples browning nicely in the sun. Every bizarre mommy/breast image that had ever passed through Ms. Behavior's mind suddenly rose to the surface, in a haunting Oedipal stew. She knew she should turn away, but like a rubbernecker at a horrible wreck, she had to go over and look. She thought about saying, "Hi, Dr. Rabinowitz-Glick. Your left breast looks like it's burning a little. Would you like me to apply some number 30 to it?" Instead, she leaned down and quietly whispered, "I am overcome with a sudden urge to put my head on your ample chest and assume the fetal position." Dr. Rabinowitz-Glick, PBD, pretending not to hear Ms. Behavior's implied distress, jumped up and greeted Ms. Behavior with a big wet kiss and a perky and burned-nipply sort of hug.

Then, of course, once Ms. Behavior was back in her home town, she had to spend the next thirteen sessions talking about how she felt about running into Dr. Rabinowitz-Glick, PBD, in Provincetown, what it meant to see her as a whole, almost naked person, and why Ms. Behavior suddenly felt like moving to Canada, or perhaps to a country in which the women are required to conceal their entire bodies except for two-inch squares of their faces.

Ms. Behavior's friend Penelope had an even weirder boundary-free lesbian therapist experience. One day when she was perusing the bookshelves in her shrink's waiting room, she spotted a paperback with her therapist's face on the cover, and, curious girl that she was, pulled it down onto her lap. Her therapist's book, which was about lesbian sexuality, immediately fell open to the most dog-eared page, and Penelope began to read. Unfortunately, this was a section of personal sexual anecdotes, which described icky details about her therapist's vagina.

"Her vagina is a moist and silky flower," Penelope reported despondently that evening. "How am I supposed to tell my therapist about my childhood issues when I know that?"

"You shouldn't have been looking through your therapist's things," Ms. Behavior suggested, in a voice she hoped was nonjudgmental.

"But if she hadn't wanted me to see it, it wouldn't have been on the bookshelf in her waiting room," Penelope pointed out.

Poor Penelope was tortured by the image of her therapist's moist and silky floral vagina during therapy for the next several months, and was left to wonder whether she should bring it up during one of her sessions. Finally, she couldn't take the tension anymore, so she worked up the courage to talk about it. Her lesbian therapist, Dr. Marilyn Lipschitz-Gould, PBD, responded by discussing her vagina further and asking Penelope whether she had ever seen her mother naked as a child.

As poor Penelope soon discovered when she expressed her distress at her therapist's response, the difficulty in confronting a boundary-free lesbian therapist is that once you finally muster up the courage to tell her that she is spilling too much, first she will tell you that you should look at your own intimacy issues, and then she'll follow the discussion with a big, sloppy, moist-and-silky hug.

This is what is really at the core of Ms. Behavior's warning; she is afraid that once your lesbian therapist turns this around, you will lose all perspective and believe that your own difficulties with intimacy are really the problem. Then you will end up spending the next five years and all of your energy trying to strip away your own boundaries, which have been deemed bad by your boundary-free lesbian therapist. You will soon become a wobbly, amoebic, boundary-less mass, just like your therapist, and then it will cost you several more years of painful self-discovery and tens of thousands of dollars before you realize that you were blessed with the ability to create protective walls around yourself for a reason.

Eventually, you will be forced to find yourself another therapist, a well-boundaried hetero one this time, who will help you to see that all the love and the light of the universe is contained within you and you are perfect just the way you are and do not need to be stripped of anything, especially not your ability to keep your emotional insides from oozing out all over. She will help you to rebuild your boundaries, so that you will be able to hold everything you need safely inside you while still letting out your feelings. It will be a beautiful experience. You can have it now, in fact, but not with a scary lesbian therapist.

Chapter Seven

✦ ✦ ✦

YOUR CERVIX
AND YOU

Sometime during your career as a lesbian, someone is going to suggest that it is a good idea that you look at your cervix. Do not be afraid. If you do not want to look deep inside yourself, Just Say No.

This lesbian-as-vaginal-explorer sentiment flourished in the seventies, when the women's self-health-care movement peaked and women began taking health care literally into their own hands. During this time, there was a bounty of educational lectures at which at least one hearty, unabashed lesbian would invariably drop her pants, hop onto a table, and, with the careful use of a speculum and a mirror, display her vagina and cervix for all the community to see. Each member of her audience would stand there feigning fascination and making small talk about cervical mucosa, unaware that the women all around were also secretly searching for the nearest exit.

Thankfully, this behavior has diminished in frequency as a group sport. However, numerous women's organizations still offer take-home plastic disposable speculums for the curious and brave (not to mention dexterous). If you are offered such a gift, do not respond with fear or revulsion, or you will reveal yourself to be hung up about your body. Just accept the offering graciously; you can always use it as a salad tosser.

If you are, however, an introspective babe actually inclined toward the gynecological equivalent of meditating on your navel, Ms. Behavior would never discourage you from doing so. The benefits of becoming familiar with your cervix and examining it on a regular basis include the possibility of recognizing any abnormality that may arise and the ability to discern changes in your cervical mucus, which can help to tell when you are ovulating (a useful piece of information if you're planning a turkey-baster baby).

However, Ms. Behavior does not think you should be forced to look at your cervix just because someone else thinks it would be neat. She should know. She will now share her own experience with cervical self-examination. Call it a cautionary tale.

Once, when Ms. Behavior was an eighteen-year-old college student, during Women's Self-Health-Care-Earth-Mother-Bounty-Moon-Solstice Week, she was offered the opportunity to join a group viewing of an acquaintance's inner life. (Helga, a large, outgoing member of the crew team, seemed only too eager to display her prized cervix.) When Ms. Behavior politely (and squeamishly) declined, she was given a take-home plastic speculum of her very own, a little pocket mirror, and a miniature flashlight. It was 1980, and looking at your cervix was considered a hip thing to do; numerous women had sworn that seeing their cervixes was somehow personally empowering, or, at the least, very fucking cool. Try as she might, Ms. Behavior could not resist. She ran home with her speculum (not in yet), got undressed, and disconnected her phone.

Ms. Behavior's take-home experience was not entirely successful, however, because just after she caught sight of her pinkish cervix, the speculum cracked and locked in an open position. (This meant that Ms. Behavior could view her cervix for a much longer time than she had originally intended.) After delicately trying to coax the speculum closed without doing herself any permanent damage, Ms. Behavior was rendered motionless in an awkward position, free to contemplate the embarrassing nature of her plight. She could not very well walk to the infirmary to get help, and although she had a phone, it was disconnected, and besides, who was she going to call? Finally, after what seemed like several days, providence and some gentle jiggling caused the speculum to close, releasing Ms. Behavior from her predicament. She tossed the nasty plastic speculum into the trash, where it belonged. (She kept the mirror and the flashlight.) Since then, only Ms. Behavior's friendly gynecologist has seen her cervix, which is fine with Ms. Behavior.

It is true that your cervix is part of who you are as a woman, but really, you have to be more objective about it than that. Although your esophagus and your intestines are part of who you are as a human, if someone offered you a take-home endoscope or a take-home sigmoidoscope, would you accept it? Ms. Behavior does not think so. So when someone approaches you eagerly, speculum in hand, offering you an opportunity for self-knowledge, do not panic. Deciding against looking at your cervix does not make you any less of a feminist or any less enlightened. And there are several creative responses at your disposal, if only you are prepared:

1. "Oh, that old thing? I've seen it more times than I can count. In fact, I've already spent all of my remaining vacation days looking up there."

2. "If I was meant to see my cervix, it wouldn't be hidden six inches up inside my vagina, or my neck would be longer, or I'd have eyes on my fingertips."

3. "I've been examining my own cervix every month for three years now. But if you'd like to show me yours, I can do a compare-and-contrast."

4. "I can't tonight. I've rented *Coal Miner's Daughter*."

Then rent *Coal Miner's Daughter*, order yourself a pizza, and go home. Take your shoes off and relax comfortably on your couch. Before you slip too far into a lovely meditative trance, remember to disconnect your phone; someone who wants to show you her cervix might be trying to call.

Chapter Eight

✦ ✦ ✦

TURKEY BASTERS, EYEDROPPERS, AND SPERM BANKS: AND BABY MAKES THREE

Having read this far, you are committed to your dyke life, Ms. Behavior suspects. (Most fly-by-night lesbians probably fled during the wimmin's music festival chapter.) So as a dedicated dyke strolling on the beaches in Provincetown or La Jolla, you have surely seen the dyke-with-tyke families making their weekly pilgrimages to the shore, dragging their Big Wheels onto the sand. By now you probably wonder if the baby-mania thing could happen to you. Ms. Behavior suspects you know the answer.

One day you are part of a regular lesbian couple, going to work every day, hanging out at home, having dinner with friends, and scoring high points in your weekly volleyball game. The next day you find yourself gazing longingly at other women's babies at the shopping mall and the grocery store, rating them in terms of their snatchability. The operative question is this: If you were the larcenous sort, how likely would you be to filch this particular chubby little baby? Soon you are giving even the snotty, drooly, whiny babies high scores.

You go through a period of babysitting a lot for your friends' kids, and don't even mind how messy it can be. Within weeks you are overtaken by an urge you don't understand, and you realize that you *must* have one. Now you are in trouble.

Ms. Behavior suggests that at first you try to ignore the maternal longings that rise like shimmering bubbles from deep within your body. They might just go away, which would save you a lot of trouble, not to mention cash. (Have you checked the prices on diapers, bottles, and baby food? Not to mention the cost of sperm, which oughtta be cheap but ain't.) If, however, the feelings linger or grow stronger during the course of at least twenty-four menstrual cycles, it's time to consider breeding.

Initially, you will keep painstaking lists of all the men you know, evaluating them in terms of their genetic worth (without informing them that they are candidates for your mission). You consider their intelligence, their looks, their family history, and, Ms. Behavior hopes, whether or not they have a sense of humor. As it turns out, most of them have some sort of fatal flaw, the metaphorical or even spiritual equivalent of chronic halitosis. (If not something superficial, like, say, an unusually prominent nose and buckteeth, then perhaps a long familial history of *total insanity*.)

You approach the one or two remaining candidates with trepidation and excitement, attempting to present your desire for their genetic material as a huge compliment. You stammer a little. They turn red and start to perspire. Even as you explain that their responsibility would begin and end with masturbating into a cup and emphasize that their prized sperm gets wasted all the time anyway, they clutch their *cajones* as if they are rare and precious gems. They apparently fear that if they do not protect themselves with their hands, you may somehow be able to extract their semen. (Perhaps they are remembering high school.)

You decide that you don't need their lousy semen and that it would be simpler and legally sounder to go through a sperm bank. You and your lover begin to pore through books describing potential donors, basically Sears, Roebuck catalogues of men. Like any wise consumer, you try to pick the donor with the coolest features and hope that you won't be duped by false advertising.

Your lover is drawn to a man of Mediterranean descent, because she, a dark-eyed Greek woman, wants the baby to have her coloring. You have your heart set on the fair-skinned Russian poet, because you want the baby to be sensitive and creative. You argue for weeks, neither willing to give in to the other. Eventually you compromise, settling on a Dutch schoolteacher who claims, in his profile, to be funny and cavity-free.

Now you take your basal body temperature every morning before dragging yourself out of bed. Some days you are still dreaming. (In one dream, you are eating a carrot, so you chew the thermometer and it breaks in your mouth.) When you go out to dinner with your friends, they comment that evaluation of your vaginal mucosa has become the center of your world and that it is no longer pleasant to eat with you. You realize that they have a point.

The first time you and your lover inseminate, you try to incorporate the process into your lovemaking — a bad idea. You try to get into the sex, but all you can think of is those little creatures swimming and whether you are doing it right or not. You wonder if your legs are high enough in the air and how long you have to stay on your back. You worry that maybe your body will reject semen as a foreign substance. You and your lover have a big fight about the correct way to do it, and $350 worth of sperm ends up staining the cotton sheets. You decide not to incorporate insemination into your lovemaking anymore.

Your mother calls you every few days, begging you to change your mind about getting pregnant. "You can still get married," she informs you. "It's never too late. Then you can have a baby the *normal* way." You tire of protesting, so you hold the phone out in the air. That way, when she complains that you're not being fair to her (because what could she possibly tell people if you do get pregnant?), you will not hear her.

Your life revolves around the timing of your reproductive system. Your calendar, thermometer, and ovulation kit become your constant companions, and eventually the instruments you relate to your bad mood. After a few months of fruitless attempts, you switch sperm donors, thinking that perhaps the Dutch schoolteacher shoots blanks. The Russian poet becomes the next candidate; you just know that if anyone can knock you up, it will be him.

Now your ordinarily mild-mannered lover is getting edgy and blaming it on *your* hormones. You know everything is really *her* fault and start sleeping in the other bedroom. Several times a week, you apologize to each other, cry, and then start all over again.

It all changes the morning you wake up, run to the bathroom, and vomit. You check your urine and the stick turns blue. Your persistence has paid off: YOU ARE PREGNANT! You and your lover are both thrilled; divorce proceedings cease abruptly. Blissfully in love once again, you cannot imagine why you ever fought. When you tell your mother she's going to be a grandmother, she looks as if she suffers from morning sickness too.

You soon get big enough to show. Strangers put their hands on your belly — nothing a good slap won't cure — and you become subjected to endless presumptuous questions. When people ask who the father is, you smile and point to your lover. Or you say "an unknown Russian poet." Or you tell them to drop dead and mind their own business. Or you look at them blankly, as if their voices are merely static interference in the music of your mind.

At first you think you will give birth at home with a sensitive lesbian midwife, who will feed you herbal tea instead of painkillers and play Enya tapes as you push the baby out into a tub filled with warm water. But you soon start having a recurrent nightmare in which you scream loudly for hours and hours and no one hears you. Your therapist explains what the dream means, and it is so obvious that you are pissed that you had to pay her eighty dollars. Now you realize that as much as you like the idea of being "natural," pain seems like a very bad idea, so you arrange to give birth in a cold, impersonal hospital where they give lots of intravenous Demerol.

Once you are heavily medicated, you have many awarenesses, which remain with you forever, as both premonitions and memories. Here is what stays with you: The day of your baby's birth is blissful and nearly pain-free. Your lover is a perfect, attentive angel who holds your hand and whispers sweet promises into your ear. The doctor is a kind, compassionate woman who never yells at you when you don't push hard enough. You scream only when the shoulders emerge. The baby pops out in thirty minutes, a beautiful chubby-cheeked, dark-skinned, creative-looking cherub. You all live happily ever after, a lovely little lesbian family unit.

Part Two

THE BOYS:
GAY RITUALS,
CULTURE, &
FASHION

Chapter Nine

✦ ✦ ✦

FINDING YOUR NICHE WITHIN THE GAY COMMUNITY

Muscle Queens, Club Kids,
Joan Crawford's Fan Club,
Urban Status Fags, ACT UP Queers,
The Boys Who Brunch, and Leather Queens

While Ms. Behavior has been subjected to the joys and rigors of lesbian life for nearly her entire existence and has participated in more aspects of lesbian culture than she cares to remember, she has never lived life as a boy homosexual. Therefore, she has had to consult with several of her lovely and cooperative boyfriends in order to prepare for this section.

Douglas, a tall, lithe homosexual who lives in Boston's fabulous South End, swears that most stereotypes about gay men are true.

"Every cultural cliché you've ever heard is real," he says, between sips of his cappuccino. "Except maybe for the stuff about gerbils."

Jake and Larry agree with Douglas. "Ms. Behavior might piss people off by categorizing them," Jake warns, "but I think it would be fair to say that in a very general way, most gay men fit into some of these broad categories."

If you are a man who is new to gay life, it is crucial to find your niche in the community, which will consist of like-minded gay men with whom to hang out. Your "big sisters" will show you around, and, depending on the kind of fag you are, will teach you makeup tips or body-building techniques (and, in rare instances, both), skills that will be essential to your identity.

But how do you know where you fit in? Well, it seems that you don't really have much choice. Just as being gay is not a choice, the *kind* of fag you are is determined by a combination of genetics and early experiences. The best advice Ms. Behavior's gaggle of homos can give you is: Don't try to control your destiny; let it evolve. If your ultimate identity is as a member of Joan Crawford's Fan Club, you can still work out and develop big biceps, but you will never, at your core, be a Muscle Queen.

MUSCLE QUEENS are the boys who got sand kicked in their faces when they were teenagers. They were called "sissy" and "faggot" and were forced to wear other boys' jockstraps on their heads in the high school locker room. Now they spend at least 40 percent of their waking hours trying, sometimes successfully, to build Charles Atlas bodies. After years of careful research, Ms. Behavior has determined that the size of a gay man's muscles is directly proportional to the degree to which he was tormented in adolescence. Each year of abuse adds another set of bench presses and stomach crunches.

Muscle Queens are not just into their own bodies; they are also obsessed with other men's physiques. But you wouldn't know it from talking to them, because conversations with Muscle Queens generally center on their own pecs, abs, and body-fat percentages. Unlike straight bodybuilders, Muscle Queens rarely talk about gorging on raw eggs and steak. (They might, however, talk about a high-carb, high-protein diet, as well as the latest exercise device Suzanne Somers is peddling on TV.) The main fact distinguishing most Muscle Queens from their straight bodybuilding counterparts is that they have memorized the anatomy charts to the point where they can name all of their muscle groups in Latin.

If you find yourself attracted to Muscle Queens (or boning up on your Latin), you should bear in mind that they never date out of their species; they are, in fact, repulsed by flabby, out-of-shape flesh and have no tolerance whatsoever for even the teensiest bit of cellulite. So if you want to date a Muscle Queen, be forewarned: You have to become one first. (Ms. Behavior hopes this won't necessitate a trip back to high school to find some kids to torture you more.)

If you don't feel tons of testosterone coursing through your veins, don't worry. In gay life, you may have noticed, being muscular is not necessarily related to being masculine. In fact, some of the biggest limp-wristed lispers are Muscle Queens, primarily for the aforementioned reason of having had to learn self-defense. It can be kind of alarming, however, to see a huge bruiser with overdeveloped muscles bench-press four hundred pounds and then wiggle over to the water cooler, fanning herself like Bette Davis.

CLUB KIDS are another species entirely. They were the small fringe of homosexuals who managed to be cool in high school, primarily because they smoked a lot of pot and participated in some so-called performance art. They did not take being called "faggot" to heart, because they had already developed a night life outside of high school, during which they hung out with older and more jaded gay men. If someone kicked sand in their faces at the beach, they went home and wrote grim poetry about it and smoked some more pot.

Club Kids are pasty-white nocturnal creatures who know the words to every disco song ever recorded. While they frequently do not have much money, because they *hate* to have to work — especially during the day, which is reserved for sleeping — they manage to get themselves on the guest lists at all the best clubs and rarely, if ever, pay for their drinks. (If they can't find someone to buy their Coronas, they mooch drink tickets from overzealous promoters who love to have good-looking Club Kids by their sides.)

Too hip to pay attention to fashion magazines, Club Kids are responsible for setting their own trends, which sometimes become mainstream. In the early nineties, they originated the perpetual appearance of caps, knapsacks, and vinyl pants, and the nostalgic resurgence of every childhood sneaker that was ever popular.

Club Kids have an impact on which performers become divas and on which stars fall with a clunk to the ground. They decide when Madonna is hot and are essentially responsible for when she becomes passé. They were into voguing and drag at least a decade before such phenomena became mainstream. They suffer from an inexplicable coolness that makes other fags uncomfortable.

They are the homosexuals most likely to develop drinking problems and to start looking old very fast. In some cases, they retire early and become members of Joan Crawford's Fan Club.

JOAN CRAWFORD QUEENS can be difficult to be with if you are not among their ranks. They spend most of their time quoting lines from black-and-white movies. An evening of fun for them consists of sitting at home with a bunch of friends wearing eye makeup and scarves on their heads, performing little segments from *Whatever Happened to Baby Jane?* If you cannot distinguish a Tallulah Bankhead line from a Bette Davis line, they will run you out of town, but not before snapping their fingers over their heads and quoting you to death.

Joan Crawford Queens have a rare talent for bitterness, and they ought to; they have spent substantial portions of their lives cultivating the fine art of bitchiness. They can quote every line from *Mommie*

Dearest, All About Eve, and *Who's Afraid of Virginia Woolf?* and many of them can *become* Joan or Bette in the blink of an eye. If you call a Joan Crawford Queen a cynic, she will take it as a compliment. In fact, one such queen petulantly informed Ms. Behavior that "a cynic is just a perfectionist who has become disappointed with the world."

The older generation of Joan Crawford's fans are also known as Nellie Queens. Their earliest media model of gay life was *The Boys in the Band,* and they easily slip into characterizations from that movie. Prone to calling each other Mary, Blanche, and Friends of Dorothy, they refer to each other in the third person only as "she" or "her." Members of this subgroup drink manhattans and wear woven sandals to show off their pedicures. They have a great appreciation for exotic headwear and can often be found wearing elaborate turbans. If you visit a Nellie Queen in the morning, you are bound to see remnants of last night's mascara.

This group is prone to melancholia and pill taking; in fact, those who are not addicted try to cultivate these symptoms, out of identification with their heroines from *Valley of the Dolls.*

The younger generation of Joan Crawford Queens are far less dramatic in their presentation but have just as much invested in the memorization and performance of their cinematic roles. And they have even more material than the older queens, because a whole new generation of campy films have come out in their day. A particular contemporary favorite seems to be *Steel Magnolias,* especially the frantic diabetic scenes.

How did the younger Joan Crawford Queens become so bitter? Probably from too many years of living with their parents, Ward and June Cleaver, who tried to make their childhoods nauseatingly middle-class "normal" while ignoring their sissy behavior. Isolated for their queerness at home, these homosexuals found refuge in old movies and Barbra Streisand songs. Most of them can also recite all the words to *Funny Girl,* and some even name their pets after the characters in *The Way We Were.* (Larry and Jake have a dog named Hubble.)

It's easy to tell if you belong with this segment of the gay community. If you cannot recite at least 60 percent of the dialogue from any version of *A Star Is Born,* go back to sleep.

Any fag from any niche can acquire characteristics of an **URBAN STATUS FAG,** but the real ones have an authentic air that cannot be duplicated. If you have not possessed at least three credit cards since before you were old enough to drink, this is not your niche.

Urban Status Fags do not just want beautiful things; they want you to know how much they paid for them. They belong to the most glamorous health club in town, drive expensive foreign cars, and own condos in the gay ghetto of whatever city they happen to live in at the moment. An Urban Status Fag always takes trips to exotic places, even if he has to work part-time as an airline reservation clerk in order to afford it.

In other words, you do not have to be wealthy to be an Urban Status Fag; you merely have to want to be rich and to have other people think that you are. This is why certain USFs buy very extravagant things at Bloomingdale's and Neiman Marcus but pay for them with money earned from their jobs waiting tables.

If you show a USF a new shirt that you bought, he will reserve judgment about whether he likes it until he checks the name on the label. His expensive sunglasses change several times per season, and if a salon offers a haircut for less than ninety dollars, he will never walk through the door.

Urban Status Fags are the homosexuals most likely to have a fag-hag following, consisting primarily of their soulmates, housewives from the suburbs.

ACT UP QUEERS are committed to fighting AIDS, but they have also developed their own stylistic culture. Perhaps their code of dress has emerged from an ideal of always appearing ready for combat. ACT UP Queers wear cutoff shorts, big black boots, and Caesar haircuts. They are offended when you call them gay rather than queer and have a penchant for being arrested for their cause. They are known to enjoy exchanging strip-search stories.

Many ACT UP Queers have pierced noses and multiple piercings on other choice anatomical parts, including but not limited to noses and nipples. They don't travel by airplane very often, because it would mean removing some of their accessories to get through the metal detectors.

When ACT UP Queers go out to clubs, they are likely to wear only underwear, with, of course, the ubiquitous black boots. They do not like to spend a lot of money on conventional clothing or jewelry. You might, however, find them picking through the trash from your garage in an attempt to find suitable adornments.

THE BOYS WHO BRUNCH live in major metropolitan areas, where they have access to the finest restaurants, nightclubs, and, if it becomes necessary, plastic surgeons. They are a composite, watered-down version of several other classifications of homosexuals: they have petite muscles from working out a little, know all the words to *Cats,* own one or two pieces of Armani clothing, and spend much of their time standing around smoky clubs without knowing the words to the songs or the divas who sing them.

The Boys Who Brunch overrate their own knowledge and connections. They think they are film-industry experts because they see two movies a week and read *Premiere* magazine. They feel a special affinity for celebrities, because they hang out at bars and restaurants where they occasionally glimpse Julia Roberts or Liam Neeson and because they are faithful page-six readers.

The Boys Who Brunch reject all signs of aging in themselves and one another. They exchange tips with their friends about moisturizers and loofas. They sleep with Tetley tea bags and cucumber slices over their eyes, and smell like skin products.

For the Boys Who Brunch, every weekend night is about proving their youthful vigor. They begin their power naps after dinner and stay asleep until midnight. They shower, douse themselves in cologne, apply just a tiny bit of mascara, and arrive, by cab, at the clubs. Hours later, they reek of X and are still dancing nonstop until dawn, which is when they make their way to the after-hours clubs.

The true highlight of their day, however, is brunch, which is when they drink their bloody Marys and make up stories about the dark and handsome men who followed them into the bathroom of the Roxy and promised them eternal love. The Boys Who Brunch like to talk but do not like to listen to each other's stories, since they know that they are all made up.

LEATHER QUEENS are the men who slip out of their daytime attire after work, Clark Kent–style, and don their second, studded skins. Prone to calling one another names like Daddy and Bear and anything preceded by Big (as in Big Jack or Big Ray), Leather Queens are often a lot less frightening than they appear.

Although some are serious about s/m, most Leather Queens are more into the fantasy and the appearance than their big black boots and basket-accentuating chaps would lead you to believe. For these men, who may actually be legal secretaries or MDs or teachers during the day, the leather is more a costume than a lifestyle. This is not to say that there aren't some Leather Queens who like nothing more than to lube up a gloved fist and go at it with someone in a harness, but rather that many more men parade in the attire than engage in the behavior.

Leather Queens are usually into body hair and natural odors. They enjoy their masculinity and love men who epitomize their hard-riding, hardworking ideals. These butch men wouldn't be caught dead eating brunch. They are much more comfortable at the takeout line at Burger King or cooking a pig over a barbecue pit.

Since they hang out in clusters of men who are like them, Leather Queens often fight about who among their crowd is the biggest top.

If you can win such an argument with a Leather Queen, you will be held in high esteem and your boots will always be kept clean.

If you're a newly out gay man and not sure where you fit in, don't despair. It will soon become amazingly clear. If it doesn't, write a letter to Ms. Behavior and tell her about yourself. She'll be happy to tell you who you are.

Chapter Ten

✦ ✦ ✦

DONNING A DRESS:
DO REAL MEN DO
DRAG?

oes the idea of dressing up in a gown and heels make you queasy? If so (and you're not a lesbian), Ms. Behavior surmises that you are either a newly out man who has not yet fully come to terms with all the potential facets of gay life or a dude suffering from Compensatory Nellie Testosterone Toxicity. In either case, you cannot possibly imagine why *any* right-minded man would purposely don women's clothing and flit around in public places. But Ms. Behavior suggests that you try not to get your panties into a knot, girlfriend. For most of your decked-out sisters, drag is about illusion and fun, not about wanting to be permanently transformed into a woman. Whether you choose to indulge the lovely fantasy only on major national holidays (such as Halloween and Wigstock) or to become a regular Marilyn Monroe impersonator at your local bar, drag can be a joyful, freeing experience. Or so Ms. Behavior hears from some of her wigged-out gay boyfriends.

Once you calm down and realize that drag is cool and expressive, you will probably want to try it at least once or twice. Since it can be expensive and even dangerous (walking on those high heels and all), Ms. Behavior is happy to provide you with tips that will make your transformation even more pleasant. Just think of Ms. Behavior as your own private flight attendant during your journey into girlishness.

The first thing you will need to do is find out where the big girls shop for shoes. In some cities there are special drag stores, where all the grand, nongenetic ladies find their footwear. Besides filling a commercial need, such boutiques provide a fun place for you to spend an afternoon, frolicking with the other excited, big-footed, deep-voiced consumers. (In terms of entertainment value, it beats the hell out of soap operas or bowling. You must remember, however, never to give any indication that you feel even remotely amused, because a black eye *will* show beneath your carefully applied makeup.)

In cities that lack such specialty stores, you must be content to find tall women's shoe stores, the places where giant women with huge feet purchase their footwear, or order your heels through the mail. (Your search will be easier if you accept from the start that you are unlikely to find size 14 rhinestone pumps at Thom McAn.)

Your dress expedition is likely to be fruitful at either a drag shop, if your city has one, or any big department store that has a section for large women (sometimes referred to, à la Tracy Turnblatt, as the Hefty Hideaway Department). The salespeople and customers at Macy's might stare as you remove slinky dresses from the racks, but you are a man with a mission and should not be intimidated by their small-minded judgment. Hold your prospective outfit up against your body in front of a mirror and ask yourself these questions: Can I get it over my head without tearing it? Does the color complement my lovely face? Am I willing to shave my chest to accommodate the low neckline? Is it *me?* If you can answer yes to all these questions, head for the nearest private dressing room. (With luck, they are unisex, so you don't have to decide.)

Here is a secret that might make Ms. Behavior the enemy of retail stores: Ms. Behavior has noticed that many of her drag-indulgent friends have found a way to get their dresses virtually for free. They just purchase their lovely gowns at a large department store, leave the tags on, and tuck them in when they go out. If they are careful not to sweat too much and manage not to get any makeup on the neckline, they return them the next day. This sort of tacky consumer behavior — which Ms. Behavior is not necessarily advocating but just presenting as an option — is familiar to Ms. Behavior, because it is exactly what the women in Ms. Behavior's suburban childhood neighborhood did when they bought dresses to wear to bar mitzvahs, since they, just like any good drag queen, would sooner die than be seen in the same dress twice. Ms. Behavior would advise against expensive purchases, though, since accidents do occasionally happen, which might prevent you from being able to return your $700 Perry Ellis beaded gown.

Your life as a drag queen, however fleeting it might be, will be easier if you can enlist the help of some friendly, experienced older sisters. In order to get recommendations about the best places to find big, beautiful gowns, for example, find a gay bar with a drag clientele, or even a club that promotes occasional drag shows. That way, you will be able to approach someone sophisticated and radiant to ask for local shopping tips.

Be careful when speaking to a drag queen. You must be very deferential and kind. Let her know that she is *queen,* and that you think she is beautiful. She is also more likely to share information with you if it is clear that you realize that you could never compete with her loveliness. Well-timed and sincere compliments will ensure a pleasant conversation. Any hint of condescension and your face is history.

Serious drag queens can also provide you with invaluable womanly hints (even more than "real" females can) and teach you to walk with your high heels on. *Never* go out in drag without having practiced wearing them at home for several hours. There is nothing tackier than a clumsy drag queen who spills her drink on others because she has not learned to walk in her shoes.

You must also rely on your sisters in drag for those essential hair and makeup tips. Ms. Behavior cautions that a first-timer should *never* try to do her own makeup, as the results are almost always disastrous. Experienced drag queens will keep you from making horrifying aesthetic errors. For example, your newfound friends will, Ms. Behavior hopes, keep you from ever wearing stewardess-blue eyeshadow. Let Ms. Behavior warn you now: Unless you want to look cheap, easy, and unbearably unsophisticated, *never* wear blue or pink eye makeup. Additionally, try not to wear colors that are obviously not found in nature (slut red, for example), and do not paint thick black dramatic lines around your eyes, which will make you look more like a nocturnal mammal than Bette Davis.

The same caution goes for hair styling and wig purchasing. Do not buy yourself large, brassy-looking hair. Try for something demure and realistic. Be sure you have someone with decent taste to accompany you, or you are liable to come out looking like Carol Channing.

Before you shop or apply your makeup, decide whether you want to look like a real woman or like a man in drag. The man-in-drag look is easier to achieve but is also tackier. This is referred to as "scag drag" by some of Ms. Behavior's friends. Someone in scag drag will not shave his chest or even his mustache and will wear ugly, ill-fitting dresses that he got from his grandmother's attic. He will use an unattractive shade of lipstick and apply the same shade to his cheeks in lieu of blush. True drag queens, those who devote their lives to their art, always aspire to look as much like women as possible.

Ms. Behavior feels the need to remind you, however, that if you value your limbs, your teeth, and your hair, *never* tell a drag queen how much she looks like a real woman. It could be a very big mistake.

Call this yet another one of Ms. Behavior's cautionary tales: Ms. Behavior, who has no record of felonies, attended a recent Halloween party, for which nearly all of the men were dressed in drag. Having a vast amount of self-acceptance, Ms. Behavior came to the party dressed as herself. She was perched quietly on a ledge about twenty feet above the huge dance floor when her friend Oogie approached and introduced her to a small, friendly man named David. David sat down on the ledge beside Ms. Behavior, shook Ms. Behavior's hand, looked into her eyes, and said, "You are really one of the most realistic-looking drag queens here. I would almost believe you were a real woman, if it were not for your excessively firm handshake." Well, Ms. Behavior accidentally slipped from her perch on the ledge and (with an unaccustomed testosterone surge) nudged David right over the edge, to watch him catapult twenty feet down onto the dance floor. Ms. Behavior is confident that her readers understand this kind of accident. Although David sprained his ankle and bruised his pretty face, he ultimately recovered. David has also become a far more tactful person, Ms. Behavior has heard through the grapevine. Ms. Behavior is always pleased and happy to hear of a person's growth in the area of etiquette.

Remember, Girlena, that the most important feature for a drag queen is genuine radiance. Ms. Behavior is convinced that drag queens were put on this earth to spread love and joy throughout the universe. When you go to a drag show, notice how many people around you are smiling. Your mission as a big lady is to be expressive and happy. Let those repressed feminine feelings, for which you were beaten up as a child, spring free. Be Marilyn Monroe or Linda Evans or even Joan Rivers for a night. And let the light within you warm those around you. It is a beautiful way to be.

Chapter Eleven

✦ ✦ ✦

HEALTH CLUB ETIQUETTE, IN THE LOCKER ROOM AND OUT

On some days, Ms. Behavior is grateful she does not have to be a gay man. This looking-hot-all-the-time thing, which extends far beyond creative dressing and grooming into the area of mondo-muscle development, would be way too much work for a languorous type like Ms. Behavior, who is quite sure she would be even less robust as a gay man than she is as a lesbian. This is not to imply that Ms. Behavior is less than lovely to look at, but rather that mascara application is currently the most aerobic activity in which she engages.

Ms. Behavior thinks it a shame that attainment of the description "hot" for gay men requires excessive perspiration and a commitment to such strenuous tasks as weightlifting and grunting out loud while bulging within the pressure of tight workout clothing. But she has also noticed that, particularly in the hipper urban areas of the country, it would be very isolating to be a gay man free of rock-hard muscles. So Ms. Behavior realizes that if she were a gay man, laziness would not be allowed, and physical suffering would be the passport to a blissful social life.

Regardless of what the Muscle Queen devotees of gym culture (or cults) may believe, health clubs are particularly scary places. Never mind the bright lights, the muscleheads, the sweat, the stench, the germs, the big machines, the loud house music. The main source of intimidation is that you are exposed to all the same cruisiness and posturing that you would find in a bar, without even the small protection that regular clothing or cocktails might afford. Who ever said that attitude could not kill?

If you are a gay man who is new to the health club scene, Ms. Behavior's ever-compassionate heart cries out for you; your self-esteem is about to plummet. When you first start working out, you will probably be at least a little flabby, so a certain amount of self-consciousness is normal, and probably even recommended. Although God loves your body just the way it is, as do your lesbian friends, gay men do not. Therefore, despite Ms. Behavior's acceptance of people of all sizes and shapes, she would urge you not to flaunt your untoned body yet (unless you can squeeze it into a flattering spandex unitard), because even though you may look like an Adonis after a few years devoted to muscle sculpting, the catty health club boys will remember your initial appearance and hold it against you for life. A hunky visitor from Italy might begin to look you over, and a bitchy queen working on his quads will lean over and say, "You should have seen him six months ago. He had the flabbiest stomach and thighs!" And there goes your lunch date.

In the beginning, in keeping with the health club caste system as well as for your personal safety, you will probably be relegated to the Nautilus section of the gym. This is where the men who are not yet built hang out. There is far less chance of injuring yourself with Nautilus equipment than with free weights, and you will not hurt the eyes of those around you, who are not quite ready to see your under-developed chest straining beneath a mere fifty-pound barbell. Also, if you stick to this section for a while, your feelings of inferiority will not be triggered as much, and you won't have to increase your psychotherapy to twice a week.

If you like the way you look when you glisten, head over to the cardiovascular section and get on the Stairmaster. You won't find any of the men with truly engorged muscles here; they refuse to risk losing valuable muscle mass by engaging in such silly endeavors. If you are a sensible homosexual, however, you know that your heart is a muscle that needs a workout too, and you are willing to achieve that toned look without going on to look like you've been shooting steroids. It is difficult to talk while on the Stairmaster, but you will develop good listening skills. (You will listen to people who are a little less vain than the ones who are lifting twice their body weight in the free weight area.)

If your gym caters to a mostly gay crowd, you will probably get to watch *Myra Breckinridge* while you sweat. Style, of course, will be one of the key factors as you work out; comfort barely counts. When cut-off jeans, vests, and workboots are in vogue, they will be worn at the health club, regardless of practical matters such as ease of movement. Your old college sweats will be unappealing to some, but Ms. Behavior believes that you should wear whatever makes you happy, without regard for other peoples' opinions. If, however, you are in hot pursuit of someone's steaming manhood, you may feel the need to look fabulous while working out. In that case, Just Do It.

Whether in the weight area or the locker room, be sure to position yourself with a wide view of all the mirrors, so that you don't miss any hot young jocks who might be stretching and glistening in another part of the room. Of course, the wider your vantage point is in terms of seeing, the better it is for being seen, too.

It can be easy to meet men in a gym, because some ordinary social conventions are unnecessary. For example, if you go out to a club at night, someone who finds you attractive might undress you with his eyes. In a health club, he doesn't have to. You are already either scantily clad or naked.

Ms. Behavior, who appreciates small tokens of privacy, such as individual shower stalls, finds the intimacy of men's locker rooms interesting and frightening. It is hard for her to imagine standing naked under a shower head next to a total stranger, because it violates every germ and boundary issue she can think of. Ms. Behavior does not mean to come off as a prude, but she does not understand this sort of closeness. Can you imagine standing naked next to someone on the subway? (If so, perhaps you're the guy who recently flashed Ms. Behavior, and she would like to have you arrested.)

These naked male-bonding conventions leave Ms. Behavior feeling baffled, but she figures that you can at least use the shower thing to your benefit and find out if someone you are interested in has good hygiene, whether his belly button is an innie or an outie, and how he might look sprawled across your Ralph Lauren sheets.

If you are the type of person who has trouble recognizing it when someone is interested in you, you might find it easier in this environment. Let's say you are naked, standing in front of your locker. The man at the other end of your row is fully dressed but just won't seem to leave. He has now tied and untied his shoes eleven or twelve times, and he keeps fumbling with his lock, even though he has already emptied the contents of his locker. In such an instance you will know that he is (a) interested in you, (b) killing time waiting for the man he is really interested in to come out of the steam room, or (c) the janitor. So smile at him. The odds of being rejected are only 66 $\frac{2}{3}$ percent.

If you're the shy type, you don't have to approach someone and think of something witty to say at a health club. You can wait until your dream man is using some equipment that seems light enough for you to lift and then ask if you can "work in" with him. That way you can be near the object of your desire, smell his sweat, hear him grunt, and see if your feelings of longing remain after a couple of sets. (Ms. Behavior truly believes that sexual attraction depends a lot on pheromones, so inhale deeply while you can.) You can watch his straining muscles and that familiar look of agony or ecstasy on his face as he thrusts the weights upward. Also, if he is a power lifter, you might get to see his erection, which sometimes inadvertently happens with a huge burst of effort. This would be considered a bonus, wouldn't it? (If he happens to be on steroids, though, his wiener is probably shriveled and tiny and not worth a peek.)

Ms. Behavior's friend the Trouser Trout met one of his boyfriends in a locker room. He got to see what he might be getting himself into (so to speak) before they even exchanged phone numbers, which kind of thrilled TT. Although that relationship ultimately ended, TT still associates the smell of sweat and chlorine with that particular boyfriend, and he patrols his health club locker room regularly in pursuit of new love.

TT also reports that sexual behavior sometimes occurs in the steam room, but he claims that he does not partake. Why is it that all of Ms. Behavior's male friends acknowledge having witnessed such conduct, but none will admit to participating? Ms. Behavior is open and accepting, and never judges her friends. She also knows that *someone* must be engaging in this mischief, if everyone has seen it, and she wants to know who it is. Will some brave and honest gay man please approach Ms. Behavior and let her know that it is he who has been touching other men in the steam room? Thank you.

Chapter Twelve

✦ ✦ ✦

MS. BEHAVIOR'S
ODE TO SISSIES

In her childhood, Ms. Behavior always befriended sissy boys, those quiet, creative types who loved to color, play with dolls, and tie their mothers' silky floral scarves over their heads in tribute to Jackie O the moment they were left at home alone. Some of the sissy boys hung together in a femme gaggle, a sure target for roving jocks with hard-ons for giving wedgies to the limp-wristed. But Ms. Behavior's closest childhood friend, Gabriel, was a cute, precocious, slightly fay boy, a lone sissy who got called "fairy" and "homo" by the other kids at school. Ms. Behavior has never forgotten how mean kids can be, and there are some nasty children she remembers from elementary school who have surely grown into beastly adults whom Ms. Behavior would still like to pummel.

Gabriel was artistic and sensitive and played Barbra Streisand songs on his piano. His high voice frequently cracked while singing "The Way We Were," and his father would mutter "faggot" under his breath in the kitchen. Gabriel also took painting classes, made macrame bracelets, and freely expressed his desire to be an actor, all of which were interpreted as sure signs of sissyhood by the other kids, who seemed to have some sort of ultrasensitive twink radar.

Gabriel liked baseball, but he broke his nose nearly every time he tried to play, and he fractured his arm a couple of times falling out of his treehouse. Still, he refused to hang out with the other boys who found gym class humiliating, and he made a point of listening to Led Zeppelin and Aerosmith instead of Aretha, the Supremes, and Patti LaBelle, who were the sissy-boy favorites. He hated being called "fem" and "faggot" and tried to prove his masculinity by wearing plaid flannel shirts and Levis like the butch boys and by making a show of chasing girls.

The pubescent Ms. Behavior was one of the girls whom Gabriel awkwardly kissed and touched on a mattress on the floor of his basement. Ms. Behavior and Gabriel both tried not to make faces while they kissed, and they sometimes ran their fingers tentatively over each other's soft skin as if they wished they could be wearing gloves. Ms. Behavior was not surprised when, at age fourteen, Gabriel announced to her that he had also been fooling around with boys. (It was at about this point that Ms. Behavior realized that perhaps her own lack of interest in Gabriel's very excitable johnson, with which she was just becoming familiar, might also be significant.)

Once Gabriel realized that he was gay, he found it hard to come out, because it meant acknowledging that those name-calling kids at school had been right. Still, his stubbornness about expressing himself had been pumped and flexed so much that he gradually eased into a refreshing flamboyancy that others eventually accepted.

The writer Frank Rose, in his essay "Sissyhood Is Powerful" (*Village Voice*, November 15, 1976), offers the following definition: "A sissy is a male who is not a man and not likely to become one." Rose, like some other gay writers and psychologists, claims that most gay men aren't sissy and most sissies aren't gay, but Ms. Behavior believes otherwise. Although her experience with this is only what might be considered anecdotal, it seems to Ms. Behavior that most gay men have been considered sissies at one point or another and most boys who start out as sweet-voiced pansies do not ultimately evolve into heterosexual men. The majority of the boys Ms. Behavior knows who collected Barbies and played house as kids are still doing so today, whether literally or metaphorically. (Her friends Jake and Larry have a Barbie collection that would turn any six-year-old girl livid with envy. Their collection is so large that they have to keep one of their Barbie dolls in the freezer; they refer to her, fully dressed and magnificent, as the Ice Queen Barbie.)

Self-assessment, upon which many sociological surveys rely, is a tricky thing. Ms. Behavior's friend Tommy-Tuna claims he was never a sissy, but it is difficult to determine how accurate his perspective might be, since he is huge, muscle-bound, and tattooed but also the faggiest man Ms. Behavior knows. At the time he denied his prissy tendencies, he was lounging in his back yard in a green floral muu-muu, sipping iced tea through a skinny red straw and frantically waving a Japanese fan around his face.

Now Ms. Behavior is about to make a confession that could have dangerous repercussions. She knows that if she were not a lesbian, her preference would be for adult sissy boys. Sissy boys are the coolest and the most attractive men. What could be more appealing than a sensitive person who can communicate, cry, cook, clean, choose your clothing, style your hair, and arrange flowers on the dining room table? The appeal of sissy boys does not seem to have been lost on straight women, either, who often befriend a few to confide in. Of course Ms. Behavior realizes that even if she lost her fervent interest in women and expressed her aberrant preference, some of her wishes for gratification would never be fulfilled, because sissy boys are not usually attracted to women. (If they were, Ms. Behavior is not sure she would be at the top of the list, since she has very few outfits worth borrowing and little patience for being the subject of elaborate hair and makeup festivities.)

What is it that is so attractive about sissies? Once they grow up to be men, they have most of the feminine qualities a lesbian might find desirable, and fewer of the liabilities. They are soft, vulnerable, design-proficient, emotive, and well read (from all those years spent with their faces in books while the other boys played sports). So okay, sissy boys might be a little bitchy at times, but it is easy just to think of it as PMS. And maybe they are a little bossy about where to place the antique armoire or what kind of flowers to grow in windowboxes, but at least they are not controlling about what foods to boycott or why you should be spending all of your free time volunteering at the nearest battered women's shelter.

Sissy boys have never been sex symbols. Social stigma and internalized homophobia have ensured that universal admiration has always been directed toward men who are straight-looking and -acting, those few homosexuals who might be allowed to play football with the heteros. Gay culture has deified the small proportion of fags who represent the same ideals that straight society has extolled forever: toughness, masculinity, and hard-bodied endurance.

But Ms. Behavior predicts a seismic shift in this aesthetic. Straight women have long known about the value of sissies, and gay men are slowly learning. In fact, like any cultural trend that gets turned on its head after years and years of excess, masculinity will lose its value as an ideal over the next decade. AIDS and other social issues have brought forth the desperate need to embrace such values as sensitivity and kindness. Ms. Behavior fully expects a sissy-boy revolution to take place sometime during the next few years, a time when love and admiration for sissy boys will reach a critical mass and they will become overwhelmingly popular and desired as friends and lovers.

The painful denial and rejection of their lovely characteristics will then no longer be necessary. Workshops on "Cultivating the Sissy Within" will be offered, and books about recovering from masculinism will be written. The pejorative sting will be removed from sissyhood, and no gay man will have to decorate in secret ever again. Gyms will be forced underground, and classes on "Running with the

Swans" will be offered. Sissyhood needs to be recognized and cele-brated as an expressive, creative, and beautiful way to be. Ms. Behav-ior hopes to see the day when men will be proud of their sissyhood, and when even those who suffer from the lack of this attribute will recognize it as something to aspire to.

Chapter Thirteen

✦ ✦ ✦

PHONE SEX, PORNO, ANONYMOUS SEX: WHEN IT COMES TO PHONE BILLS, IS BIGGER BETTER?

*N*ow that nearly everyone is in twelve-step confessional mode or knows someone who is, Ms. Behavior has noticed that it is cool to admit that your life is out of control and that you had to sell your dining room furniture to pay last month's $400 phone bill, most of which was calls to chat lines. You feel especially hip if you are the first at a cocktail party to lament that you had to have a block put on your phone so that you can no longer call the 900 numbers. Go ahead, say it: "We admitted that we were powerless over phone sex, and that our lives had become unmanageable." Aaahhh. That feels better now, doesn't it?

When Ma Bell copywriters first created the ads saying "It's the next best thing to being there," they may not have had sweaty, grunty phone sex in mind. But why not? In phone sex, your erotic imagination is unleashed in a safe and friendly context. You can keep what you want, the hot and glamorous aspects of sex, and leave out the literal and figurative blemishes. (Ms. Behavior is happy to report that fiber optics generally filter out things like bad hair and body odor, unless you happen to want that to be part of the fantasy.)

Like its more technologically advanced younger sister, cybersex, phone sex allows you to dabble in ideals that no real person could possibly match. You allow another person's voice to transport you to the freest, most passionate corner of your mind. You can undress in utter darkness or in the radiant and accepting glow of your lover's eyes. Although your trick might really be a three-headed toad, who cares? Your imagination allows him to be a tall, exotic Adonis who wants nothing more than your total pleasure. Or a tough-talking cowboy who will treat you like a bronco that needs to be broken, if that's what you want. And you don't have to think much about your own behavior, either; you can be sweet and tender or rough and fast, without the emotional baggage that comes with allowing someone to infiltrate your home.

Perhaps the most appealing aspect of phone sex is its safety; it will not transmit diseases or put you in the physical company of unsavory people, not to mention the occasional psychopath. Psychopaths can be found on the phone lines, of course, but at least you don't have to tell them where you live. The bottom line with phone sex is that you maintain ultimate control: You can hang up at any time. (Ms. Behavior does not mean this to sound like an advertisement for phone sex. If it does, she wishes to be paid as much as Candice Bergen is for those Sprint commercials. Thank you.)

If there is one cardinal rule for phone sex, however, it is this: Resist the temptation to meet anyone in person. You will be crushed by disappointment. This man you envisioned as Fabio actually resembles Barney, which will initiate a cycle of despair that looks like this: You think that you should try meeting someone from the phone lines one more time, because statistical probability suggests that the next one might be normal or at least cute. But you meet more and more droolers and weirdos and men who act like Mr. Rogers, until you start to think that there must be something wrong with people who indulge in this form of socializing, that these are the desperate losers of the universe, the men who are unable ever to get dates. And then you realize that you have been doing it too, so you get depressed, because you start to suspect that you might be a loser.

Never mind the money you've spent or the feeling of compulsion that your phone sexploits have triggered. Never mind the fact that you spend all your time dialing 1–900-HOT-BEEF at the expense of having a real social life or being with your friends. Forget about the fact that you haven't seen a movie in months or planted flowers in your garden. The isolation that this activity causes in your life, the separation from humanity, is not what upsets you. It is the I-might-really-be-a-pathetic-dweeb feeling that finally compels you to call AT&T to put a block on your phone. It is the fact that when you look in the mirror, the image reflected at you is of all the scrawny, mossy-toothed geeks you used to push around in high school.

Like most of the lovers you have had trouble leaving, phone sex turns out to be one of those things that you cannot live with and you cannot live without. You think cold turkey might be the best method of quitting. You pick up smoking instead.

Once you stop dialing, time ceases to move forward. You were spending so much of it on the phone that without that chatter, your life feels empty and even more depressing. Soon this level of depression makes you hide from your friends, and dating people in real life no longer even seems like an option. Now you find yourself in the X-rated section of the video store, skulking around with the other degenerates, trying to find a new version of the old and tired *Hot Young Jocks* video. You can never find the video you want, because people hide the boxes so that no one else can rent the film for which they are waiting. (This is inside information from Ms. Behavior's friend Jake, who works in a video store.) So not only have you been reduced to a solitary sex life, you also suffer the humiliation of finding that your only accompanying tools have become the really dull movies with the Danny DeVito look-alike actors. In order to keep yourself from slipping even deeper into depression, you convince yourself that Danny DeVito is actually not so bad. Now your friends begin to worry. So does Ms. Behavior.

You think back to your glorious old days of strolling along the beach looking for fabulous men with whom to have hot safer sex. You remember that some of the men were not bad-looking and that there was an excitement about having sex outdoors. You put on your cutest shorts and combat boots and practice strutting in front of your mirror and think of how nice it will feel to have the wind blow through your hair as you cruise the dunes. Then you remember the poison ivy and just how long it took for that rash to clear up. You remember your phobia about Lyme disease, and how you made all your friends search every inch of your body for ticks every time you returned from the beach. You take your combat boots off and lie down on your bed to stare at the cracks on the ceiling.

It is in this position, lying on your back and looking up toward the heavens, that you have a spiritual awakening. As you let the feeling overtake you, your whole body warms and relaxes. As soon as you feel ready to stand up, you reach for the phone and bring it back to your bed. Your first call is to the phone company, to ask it to remove the block on your line.

Chapter Fourteen

✦ ✦ ✦

SIZE QUEENS

Some gay men say size doesn't matter. It is Ms. Behavior's suspicion that these people are (a) highly evolved and sensitive men who have moved on to much deeper and more important issues, (b) petitely endowed themselves, or (c) lying.

It is bad enough to grow up being female, with all of the comparisons about breasts and weight and figures and cellulite. But growing up as a man in a culture that emphasizes *big* things, like big money, big homes, big cars, and big muscles, makes it very hard to have anything other than an extra-large schlong. It is for this reason that Ms. Behavior extends her sincere sympathy and kindest wishes to her more modestly endowed male readers. She wants you to know that she accepts you just the way you are and loves you for your expansive inner self. She knows that your soul is beautiful and feels certain that your tiny, meager penis is just fine as is. And no, you don't have to show it to her to convince her of anything.

If you happen to have a honking big one, Ms. Behavior extends her congratulations but wants you to know that she is not really impressed. Your good fortune is based on genetics, not on anything you have done to deserve it (unless you really take that karmic stuff over the top and believe that it is due to some sort of magnanimous behavior in a previous incarnation, which Ms. Behavior thinks unlikely). Your hugeness will not cause Ms. Behavior to treat you in any special way; to her, it is no different from your happening to have a big nose.

It is hard to know when preoccupation with size begins, but Ms. Behavior knows it sometimes happens quite early. She remembers at age fourteen watching her young poofter friend Gabriel adjust his johnson inside his bikini briefs to point upward so that it would look more substantial. Gabriel also whipped out his ruler one day and measured it, right in front of the too-cool-to-be-astonished Ms. Behavior. At first he agonized over whether it was correct to measure it from the top or from underneath (which would add some length). In a generous mood (and also ill equipped to deal with massive teenage insecurity), Ms. Behavior kindly suggested that he measure it from below. "Six inches," Gabriel said proudly as he removed the ruler from beneath his erection. "And I'm not even full-grown yet!"

Years later, when Ms. Behavior danced with her friend Oogie at a tea dance in Provincetown, she saw a wadded-up pair of socks fall out of the leg of his shorts and hit the dance floor. At first Oogie pretended not to notice, hoping that she had missed it. Ms. Behavior smiled at Oogie, letting him know that she offered only acceptance and love. Oogie just smiled back and shrugged. "I'm a grower, not a shower," he explained, reaching down and scooping up his footwear. "I look really small until I get hard, so I need all the help I can get."

Ms. Behavior, sensing Oogie's embarrassment, attempted to offer a few words of comfort. "I hear it's not the size of the prize," she said, "but the motion of the ocean." Oogie seemed relieved.

If you are not humongous of member, take heart. Ms. Behavior has found that some men actually appreciate average-size wieners. While they might think big is beautiful in terms of appearance, they have less appreciation for enormity in terms of function. As Ms. Behavior's friend Kenny, ever the pragmatist, says, "Big is nice to look at and to play with, but you can't *do* anything with it. Give me an average one any day."

Still, the cultural obsession with hugeness would make it appear not only that bigger is better but also that there are slim pickings for men who appreciate average endowment. No one seems to admit to being regular. At the risk of sounding penis-fascinated and losing her already shaky standing in the lesbian community, Ms. Behavior could not help but notice during her serious, committed research to this topic how many personal ads are written by men who claim to possess eight or more inches of manhood, and who sometimes also include circumference measurements that are larger than those of beer cans. In these personal ads, it would appear that huge is usual. But if six inches is average according to sexuality researchers (and Ms. Behavior's independent telephone poll), what has happened to all the men in that "normal" range? Are they all living on the Island of Mediocrity? Plus, isn't anyone *small?* Where are all the three- and four-inchers? Are they hiding, hanging their various heads in shame? Are they trapped in Munchkinland?

Ms. Behavior believes that we should aspire to make gay and lesbian culture safe for men and women of all sizes and shapes. She believes that once we evolve into a suitably nurturing and accepting community, Men With Petite Rods will have their own floats in the Gay Pride march. *Blue Boy* will feature Lilliputian month, and *Honcho* will have big and small men mixed together as centerfolds. Until that time, Ms. Behavior urges the small of penis to come out and take your place as upstanding members of the community.

Chapter Fifteen

✦ ✦ ✦

WHAT'S THE BIG DEAL ABOUT BODY HAIR?

As hard as Ms. Behavior has tried, she cannot understand the big deal about body hair. She can see being attracted to someone for the brightness of his eyes, the fullness of his mouth, the kindness of his expression, or even the bulge of his, uh, wallet, but how could you possibly choose a date or build a relationship on the basis of a bunch of wiry, insignificant, vestigial little hairs?

In one tale of hair love, Ms. Behavior's friend Corey met his last boyfriend, Alex, on the beach when Alex approached him after noticing that he had "perfect hair alignment." In a thirty-minute conversation that Ms. Behavior now regrets, Alex attempted to explain to Ms. Behavior why he found the shape, style, and growth patterns of Corey's body hair to be so alluring. He spoke of it the way a designer would talk about acquiring the perfect painting, the way a lover would speak of the sweet rise and fall of his beloved's chest in the morning. As Alex spoke, his long fingers stroked imaginary hair and got tangled in the nest of a pretend-lover's stomach hair. He drew careful pictures of perfect hair swirls, explained which patterns of growth are most desirable, and described the texture and color of the body hair of each of his previous lovers at great length. As someone who was just beginning to examine this phenomenon, Ms. Behavior realized that talking with Alex about the relevance of body hair was like listening to a foot fetishist extol the virtues of clipping your toenails in a straight line. Besides, the mental picture with which Ms. Behavior was left was defaced by Alex's drooling. (So was his drawing.)

If you doubt that some men seek happiness based on body hair, you need only read the personals to see otherwise. You might be amazed at how many of the advertisers refer to wanting someone who is excessively hairy, bald as the moon, or totally shaven ("Little cub seeks big, hairy daddy bear for hot forest encounters and possible long relationship. Send a note and a photo of your body hair, as well as a sample patch taken from your pecs"). Never mind an interest in film or literature, or even jogging, for that matter. It is those dark, curly, pubic-type hairs (or lack of them) that drives these men wild.

Now that toned and muscular bodies have become de rigueur, a subculture of hairless gay men has also evolved. Although some men who remove their hair are bodybuilders hoping to display their muscle definition, they are far outnumbered by random homosexuals who merely hoist ten-pound dumbbells twice a week and shave or wax to emphasize the microscopic bulges they have cultivated. Watch their hairless quadriceps strain as they forcefully press against fifty pounds of steel with their Nike hightops!

In case you are hoping to achieve that hairless Vegas showgirl appearance yourself, Ms. Behavior must warn you about the risks of using chemical depilatories. Besides filling your bathroom with a foul odor, they may make your chest and genital area break out in a bumpy red rash and can make your hair grow back in sharp little spikes which will impale your tricks and make them scream in pain. No one will be anxious to rub his soft, smooth skin against the rough, penetrating barbs rising out of your pores.

Head hair or the lack of it is perhaps a less dangerous obsession. If you find that your skull is beginning to reflect the light of the sun, Ms. Behavior suggests that you leave it that way. Nearly all toupees and hair weaves are inauthentic and embarrassing. If you think people won't notice a big blob of synthetic hair on your head, you're wrong. You should especially not underestimate your gay sisters, who never miss anything.

If you insist on buying a toupee despite Ms. Behavior's advice to the contrary, buy an expensive and realistic one and don't tell anyone, especially not a gay man, because then *everyone* will know. Do not spray-paint your bald spot with one of those ridiculous cans of brown paint that are advertised on TV in the middle of the night. If it rains, you are doomed.

Who would have thought hair fetishes could have so many possible manifestations? When Ms. Behavior's friend Oogie was in his late teens, he met an older man who liked to play barber. Oogie merely had to sit in a chair in the man's kitchen and allow the *faux* barber to give him a haircut and shave. Oogie was allowed to watch TV while the man clipped and made sighing noises. Even better, he was paid twenty-five dollars each time, just to be the recipient of an amateurish haircut. Sometimes he just had to call the barber on the phone and describe his short, bristly hair. Oogie is now attracted only to bald men, which Ms. Behavior suspects is because this experience is indelibly imprinted on his psyche in some twisted fashion, but Oogie swears it is unrelated.

The hair phenomenon that fascinates Ms. Behavior most, however, is ball shaving. Ms. Behavior remains sad that she has never been invited to attend a ball-shaving party. She can envision men sprawled out on various couches throughout an apartment, languishing in clusters of three or four, each awaiting the tender application of Gillette shaving cream to his sensitive orbs. She has heard, too, about the sighs of pleasure and apprehension that fill the room, and about the delicate strokes with which the hair is removed with a dangerous straight razor. (Oogie insists that straight razors are actually preferable, and he should know. He once let his friend Paul shave him with an electic hair clipper, which left his nuts "chewed up.")

Even gay porn stars have smoothly shaved balls, to the point where hairiness looks practically abnormal. Why has testicle shaving become such a way of life among gay men?

"Shaved balls look bigger and feel better against your face," according to Ms. Behavior's friend Steve.

"And you don't get a mouthful of hair when you lick them," Kenny added.

Ms. Behavior asked no further questions.

Some physical preferences are easy to understand in terms of attraction, and others seem totally weird. Ms. Behavior believes that certain aesthetic desires can be accepted at face value and others are buried deep within the fetishist's unconscious. An attraction to men with dark eyes and hair, for example, may be just that or may hark back to an early movie-star fantasy. But Ms. Behavior has found that most aesthetic preferences that have a quantitative focus (including such things as hair, age, money, and size) go beyond their surface meaning and represent some sort of deeper psychological issue. Ms. Behavior will not extend her research into the lush jungle of the hair fetishist's psyche; she feels that psychoanalysts are already paid too much for too little work, so she will leave this area of analysis open for their investigation.

At this point some of Ms. Behavior's readers may be wishing for a way to capitalize on this information so that hair fetishists will fall in love with them. For such greedy types, Ms. Behavior will offer advice on how to become more attractive to men who are preoccupied with hair.

Fetishes are usually about exaggeration, taking something that exists in an ordinary realm over the top. If, for example, you are partially bald, with just a rim of hair around the perimeter of your head, you will be much more likely to attract men who love baldies if you just shave that silly little ring of remaining hair. Suddenly you go from looking like any old middle-aged man named Stanley to having the shiny-headed mystique formerly available only to such icons of manhood as Mr. Kleen and Kojak. If you happen to have only a few hairs on your chest or pubic area, you could just shave the remaining ones, for that smooth and nubile look associated with youth and innocence.

Conversely, if you are pretty hairy and you want to attract men who love bears, you need to wear clothing that will emphasize your hairiness. Try wearing shirts with low necks, above which your dark tufts of manliness can poke. Condition and moisturize your body hair for that extra-shiny emphasis that will attract further admiration. (Ms. Behavior must caution here that if you are small, thin, pale, and hirsute, this will not be a good look.) Run your fingers through your hair and puff it up, teasing it into a pleasing style. Blow it dry while rubbing in some mousse. Just bear in mind that if you exaggerate your hairiness, your admirers will expect very manly behavior. They will want you to protect and care for them in a beastly way. They may expect you to wear a loincloth and play games in which you are King of the Jungle. You will love it.

For those of you who have only an ordinary amount of head and body hair, not too much or too little, Ms. Behavior is sympathetic. You will have to find another device through which to find true love. Although you are surely feeling sorry for yourself now, Ms. Behavior would like to point out that if you cannot depend on your hair, you will have to develop your other charms, which may in the end make you a happier, more well-rounded person.

Chapter Sixteen

✦ ✦ ✦

THIS THING OF
BEAUTY ALSO HAS
THE GRACE OF GOOD
TASTE

*M*s. Behavior loves to visit her friends Tom and Steve for the holidays, because their linen napkins are always folded into swan shapes, with the napkin rings wrapped tightly around their long graceful necks. Plus, the center of the table is likely to be adorned with a bowl filled with slow-swimming, multicolored tropical fish and long stems of fragrant flowers bursting with fresh buds.

Ms. Behavior looks around the room, first at the gleaming hardwood floors and then at the lacy antique-white swags and jabots. No matter how frequently she visits, there is always some new and charming touch — an exotic ceramic mask, a lovely framed lithograph, a sprig of fresh freesia. Everything is so neat, so airy. Tom comes scurrying out of the kitchen with drinks in Baccarat crystal glasses on a sterling tray, while Steve sets the table with his antique Wedgwood china. By the time the caviar is served, Ms. Behavior's mind has wandered to her own living room, where books and papers are piled knee-high and discarded socks litter the carpet. She thinks about the empty Tylenol bottles next to her bed and the mugs that are filled with herbal tea and mold spores. By the time she remembers her kitchen sink, she is depressed. If she looks over into Tom and Steve's beautifully decorated, sun-filled, recently-featured-in-the-pages-of-Metropolitan-Home living room, she might barf into her vichyssoise.

Why is it that neither lesbians nor hetero couples have the talent for creating such exquisite environments? Ms. Behavior can recall several instances in which she met dykes or straight people who had incredibly well decorated apartments, and she remembers being excited, thinking she was discovering a new and deviant trend. Unfortunately, Ms. Behavior was disappointed each time to learn ultimately that these people who had appeared to be design-gifted had merely hired gay male decorators.

In an attempt to understand this phenomenon, Ms. Behavior consulted her friend Douglas, a fabulous gay decorator who was beaten up in seventh grade for subscribing to *Architectural Digest* and *Women's Wear Daily* and for hanging curtains in his treehouse.

"I think we are all trying to imitate the queen of England," says Douglas, pouring himself a cup of tea from an ornate china teapot. Douglas's theory is that some gay men are trying to be accepted where they may not have been as adolescents. "We are overcompensating by decorating our lives," he claims. "Like, I am a good person because I have a Fabergé egg."

Douglas's lover, Roberto, says that he does not know whether the gay male taste thing is innate or culturally indoctrinated, although he is aware that he identified more with Donna Reed than with her husband. "Perhaps it is about falling for the homemaker mystique and making a comfy place for hubby to come home to," he says, gently kissing Douglas's triceps.

Ms. Behavior understands that the gay design aesthetic extends beyond personal proclivity and has become a social activity and a means of bonding. Instead of calling each other to process the last period of the hockey game, a bizarre straight-male bonding ritual, Ms. Behavior's gay boyfriends call each other if a particularly cheesy *Dynasty* rerun or *Melrose Place* episode is on. They are invariably far more focused on what the women are wearing or on changes in the furnishings of the house than on noticing the good-looking men. "Oh, look what Krystle's got on," they squeal. "She wore that a few weeks ago, and it looks like she cleaned her oven in it."

There is also a cathartic, emotive aspect of the decorating-bonding thing that can be almost . . . well, manly. One acquaintance of Ms. Behavior's hosts a Miss America Pageant party each year. The guests do not themselves dress as participants but sit in front of the TV and dish as the contestants emerge to display their dresses and talents. The thirty gay men who go to watch the pageant howl and cheer louder than anything you might hear at any Irish pub on Super Bowl Sunday. A blindfolded passerby might even assume it actually was a sporting event that these men were watching, based on the scent of excited perspiration in the air. (Ms. Behavior wonders, too, if this enthusiastic bonding behavior is really any different in essence from that of the straight Iron John men who gather with their drums to chant and yell and burp and feel a deep connection to the pungent soil and one another.)

Additionally, the men who participate in the Miss America obsession are as knowledgeable about the statistics as straight men are about sports. They can tell you which contestant won in 1974 and what she did for the talent segment. They can also provide a long-term historical perspective about such things as when the contestants began to have to do their own hair and makeup and when and why the swimsuit sponsor changed. When Ms. Behavior's friend Larry died this year, the pageant was a major topic of discussion at his memorial service, because his love and devotion for this event were so great.

Beauty pageants are not the only "holidays" worthy of excessive gay celebration. Christmas is a very festive time for Queens with Taste, whose holiday decorating notions are in direct opposition to the architect Mies Van Der Rohe's notion that less is more. In fact, it is clear from looking at the average queen's Christmas tree that *more* is actually more. The decorations are not the kind you can buy in a twenty-four-pack at Woolworth's. They are more likely to be elegant artistic pieces purchased at Tiffany's or collector's items carefully culled from endless weekend car trips to faggy antique enclaves. Tasteful ornaments are carefully placed and tree lights are always white. (Decorating a tree with tinsel is a cardinal sin, culminating in severe and permanent ostracism from the community of tasteful homosexuals.)

Ms. Behavior would, however, like to rectify the rumor that *all* gay men have good taste. Some seem to have been born with a mutated taste gene, and very little can be done to help them. These poor unfortunates have internalized the societal expectation that they be design-proficient but frequently are the last to know that they just don't have it. It is particularly amusing to see what they come up with when straight friends ask for their help in decorating. The straight friends ignore the fact that the results are hideous, because they think if their place was decorated by a fag, it *must* be fabulous. They think perhaps they just cannot see the subtle beauty, and leave ghastly decorations in place for years.

Homosexuals with no taste are very sad cases. Luckily, they have each other for comfort, because the Queens with Taste would only torture and banish them. The taste-free boys decorate in black lacquer and silver, with teal leather couches and pickled white floors. They buy all their clothing at Chess King and think that the up-the-butt thong on page 13 of the International Male catalogue was created just for them. They wear jazz shoes like the straight boys from the suburbs, and favor shag Chippendale's haircuts, which look a lot like lesbian haircut #3 but without as much frosting.

Far worse, however, than the innocent taste-free boys who don't seem to know better are the ones who have no taste but shout and scream because they think they have plenty. These homos overdo it in every realm, with lots of gold jewelry, fake Gianni Versace silk print shirts, and pseudo-Italian loafers. Their lack of taste has sometimes been attributed to cologne poisoning. They usually drive black Trans Ams with blaring radios and wear tight pants. Someone needs to tell them that they are all wrong. Ms. Behavior has subtly offered some corrective tips on an occasion or two, but now she thinks all of their concerned brothers and sisters should get together and let them know. It would be inhumane to let them go on without some loving guidance.

If you yourself have come to realize, after reading this, that you have reprehensible taste, pat yourself on the back for acknowledging it. Admitting that you are powerless over tackiness and that your life has become unmanageable will be the first step toward attempted recovery. Ms. Behavior must acknowledge that not everyone recovers from tastelessness, because there are those who are constitutionally incapable of an elegant aesthetic. In your most honest moment, however, get on your knees and pray for the willingness to have your garishness removed. Perhaps a miracle will occur.

In the meantime, try to find a Queen with Taste to take you under his wing. This person might be able to teach you how to understand, appreciate, and remember beauty. Bear in mind, though, that not everyone is trainable. Queens with Taste have laser eyes and photographic memories. When they see something they admire, whether in person or in a film, they have an uncanny ability to remember it. They can close their eyes and describe in infinite detail exactly how a room was decorated or how each person at a party was dressed. It is all retained and absorbed, ready to be tapped for later use. This is why you can go to a QWT's apartment and see a bedroom that looks just like the one in *Mommie Dearest*. This ambitious queen saw the movie a decade ago, coveted the glass closet doors lined with brass, and promised himself that someday they would be his.

Remember to be nice to your aesthetic trainer, because he is the only hope you have. A homosexual with no taste is a very sad thing. Ms. Behavior wants nothing more than to deliver you from that lonely fate. She truly prays that artistic salvation will be yours.

Part Three

GAY & LESBIAN
CULTURAL ODDITIES
THAT MS. BEHAVIOR
FINDS PARTICULARLY
COMPELLING

Chapter Seventeen

✦ ✦ ✦

TATTOOS, TATTOOS, TATTOOS, AND WHAT'S WITH ALL THIS NIPPLE PIERCING?

*M*s. Behavior will cut to the quick for you: Although she is always curious enough to research the issues she writes about, she is not always tempted to join in the rituals. (This is probably a good thing, because Ms. Behavior has sometimes written about a bunch of weird and gooey behaviors.) Participation in cybersex is one way to reveal devotion to a thorough exploration of a topic, and Ms. Behavior willingly suffered through that trying experience; a thick needle pushing through one's flesh is quite another thing. In the instances of piercing and tattooing, Ms. Behavior has willingly forgone partaking and instead settled for intensely concentrated observation.

The first time Ms. Behavior witnessed a piercing, it was of a sixteen-year-old's navel. The piercer, a severe-looking woman named Wanda who had eleven piercings of her own, including both nipples and both nostrils, liked to say things like "Pain can be such a relief." Ms. Behavior felt a little squeamish as she watched Wanda carefully lay out her implements and antibacterial ointments, explaining each step patiently, like a kindergarten teacher gone bad. The baby dyke confessed that she was getting her belly button pierced because she thought it would be cool to be the first among her friends who had pierced that particular part of her body. As the needle pushed through the skin just above her navel, she sucked in her breath but did not whimper. Ms. Behavior screamed, fell backward onto the couch, and passed out. Wanda did not invite her to witness any subsequent piercings.

Once the domain of people who wore leather G-strings and danced in cages at discos, piercing has now become fashionable among even the most mild-mannered homosexuals. Ms. Behavior's friend Oogie, a quiet, bookish, Woody Allen type, showed up at a party and removed his shirt proudly to reveal a heavy silver hoop hanging from his small pink nipple. Lots of people said ooh and aah, and then some stripped off their clothing too, to display their own lovely piercings. Ms. Behavior had to go lie down.

Talk about stupid questions: Ms. Behavior has noticed that the most frequent thoughtless thing people say when gazing at a fresh piercing or a newly scabbed tattoo is "Did it hurt?" The obvious answer to that question is an unequivocal *"YES!!!"* The degree of pain in piercing, according to Wanda, depends on the body part being pierced. An ear, a nose, or an eyebrow will obviously hurt less than a nipple, a labium, or a penis. And Ms. Behavior is not willing to contemplate the degree of pain involved in piercing one's tongue, even if you promise to fetch her some smelling salts and fan her with palm leaves.

Some trends should never be allowed to make the leap from quiet countercultural backwater proclivity to mainstream trendiness. Tattoos, for example, should have forever remained the province of only the butchest of sailors. Ms. Behavior is convinced that people who get tattooed suffer from the misguided belief that they will stay young forever. Such people clearly have no concept of how a colorful rendering of Sappho on their inner thigh might look on their eightieth birthday. And why is it that social scientists have not yet offered suggestions for how we might prepare for the sight of octogenarians with labryses and pink triangles tattooed on their faces?

Ms. Behavior does hate to sound like your mother, but she advises you to ask yourself this question before you get a tattoo: If this tattoo were a shirt, would I want to wear it every day for the rest of my life? She also urges you to consider careful placement of your lovely design. If you get tattooed in the winter, for example, think about what you might want to wear to work in the summer and whether or not you are seeking admiration of your creative expressions.

Also, Ms. Behavior hates to be less than optimistic, but she would feel remiss in not offering this caution: No matter how in love you might feel, no matter how convinced you are that this lover is the one for you forever, *never* get your lover's name tattooed on your body. Is this clear, or will Ms. Behavior have to yell? It looks tacky to have a name crossed out on your arm or your buttocks, or even to have it woven into the center of an elaborate tattooed flower patch, under the erroneous assumption that no one can still read "I love Vanessa forever" within the tiger lily. You must accept the fact that even the most fabulously and rapturously loving couples break up, and that it might be a real downer to have your ex's name lurking around your body permanently. (If you need further convincing, just ask Roseanne Arnold.)

At some point you will probably be confronted with the dilemma of what to say to a friend who proudly displays a tattoo of a pumpkin on his chest or a unicorn on her buttock. You might even be confronted with having to respond to a friend's pierced tongue or labia. Ms. Behavior finds it unnecessary to lie or feign appreciation, but suggests that you refrain from expressing disgust unless you absolutely must. This is not out of mere politeness but out of a concern for saving your emphatic expressions for issues that really matter. If you become the kind of person who wantonly expresses revulsion, your opinion on serious matters loses its impact. So a quiet one-word comment like "Wow" or "Hmmm" or "Uh-huh" will generally suffice as a nonjudgmental but nonapproving response. (Ms. Behavior's friend Penelope, a renowned psychologist, recommends "I see.")

Why have piercing and tattooing become so ridiculously popular? Why is it that people who turn white at the thought of a dental visit or who need extra therapy the week of their gynecological appointment willingly allow a self-proclaimed piercing expert to push a sharp needle through a sensitive body part or allow a picture to be emblazoned in their flesh?

All of the answers Ms. Behavior dug up in her painstaking research boiled down to the same basic concept, an idea that goes back decades and centuries and millennia: coolness.

Coolness has always been problematic. The desire to express it has resulted in many ghastly fashion trends as well as some reprehensible behavior. Ms. Behavior is happy to support you fully, however, if your own personal coolness extends only so far as the kind of fashion that can be removed before bed and does not cause pain or injury to your body. So if you like donning a particular type of footwear that makes you feel hip, feel free to stick with that. If a particular hairstyle gives you that happening feeling, go with it. Just remember, though, when someone tells you that pain is a ritual with a soothing quality, you can say that you have had enough soothing in your life. With eternal love and acceptance, Ms. Behavior reminds you: It is never too late to Say No to Pins and Needles.

Chapter Eighteen

✦ ✦ ✦

MS. BEHAVIOR EXPLORES THE TEMPTATIONS OF VIRTUAL SENSUALITY AND ISSUES A SENSIBLE WARNING

*M*s. Behavior would like to remind you that if you never eat a single fruit from the forbidden tree, you will not be tempted to strip the tree bare and greedily binge until your body bloats and bursts.

It was never Ms. Behavior's idea to become a cyberslut; it just happened that way. One day her friend Beth came over with a new computer program, hooked it up to a modem, and showed Ms. Behavior all the cool things you can do online. These innocuous tasks included making airline reservations and checking stock quotes, which Ms. Behavior thought was mildly entertaining. After Beth left for work, however, Ms. Behavior dropped into the chat area of the service and noticed a list of intriguing headings, including one called Women4Women.

Well, within seconds after signing on as Peaches123 (don't ask why), Ms. Behavior received an onslaught of tawdry messages on her screen, which said things like "Are you fuzzy and juicy?," "I really love your Peaches, want to shake your tree," and "Please come into a private room with me for a shared hot fantasy." This confused and surprised the demure Ms. Behavior, who had never before witnessed this aspect of lesbian life: women, in the anonymity of their own homes, inviting other women — virtual strangers — to engage in mutual sexual fantasy.

Since Ms. Behavior is surprisingly shy in response to overt seduction of any sort, she quickly turned the computer off and ran from the room, as if the people sending the provocative messages could see her. She hid in a corner of her bedroom, with the eerie feeling of having been seen naked by a gang of lesbians peeking through the window. In a matter of moments, however, curiosity (or something) got the better of her, and she planted herself in front of the computer and signed on again.

You must know by now that Ms. Behavior is willing to do nearly anything in the name of research, the better to serve her devoted lesbian and gay audience, the people she loves most. It was with this in mind that Ms. Behavior began to conduct an exploration of the world of virtual sensuality (a more genteel name for computer sex, which she got from her new online friend CyberCyndi). At first Ms. Behavior merely "watched" as gaggles of lesbians flattered and seduced one another, as many as twenty-three at a time in each imaginary room. The names of each of the participants (or voyeurs) in each room were listed at the top of the screen; many of the women had names like SexySuzie and HotCherry and profiles that included their occupations, hobbies, and pushup-bra sizes.

After watching numerous women from all around the country

talk about one another's panties and breasts for several long hours of painstaking attention, Ms. Behavior came to the realization that most good research involves participation. After all, she asked herself, would Timothy Leary's work have been as interesting if he had never ingested LSD? Would Mother Teresa have developed such deep compassion without living among the people she served? Besides, it has always been Ms. Behavior's goal to approach her work in the spirit of selfless giving. What better opportunity would she have to give to her readers than to submit to the rigors of participation in cybersex?

All she had to do to participate was to answer the instant messages that appeared on her screen, inviting her to enter private rooms (a place in cyberspace where you have a one-on-one, typically sexual conversation, which often culminates in practicing one-handed typing techniques). Before Ms. Behavior started, she changed her name to Monique, which turned out to be far less popular than Peaches but more reasonable in terms of the messages it inspired from lusty women. Changing her personal quote to "You've been a bad girl. Come to my room" drew lots of action from women who wished to be dominated, which amused the ordinarily less-than-toplike Ms. Behavior. She also soon found, much to her lesbian dismay, that some of the women with whom she began to exchange virtual fantasies were actually men. (The clue that tipped her off was that once they had lured her into a private room, they began to discuss aspects of their anatomy that sounded rather unfamiliar to Ms. Behavior.) This was a little disturbing.

It was Luscious77, however, who changed everything. She wrote such hot private-room fantasies that Ms. Behavior found herself shivering with perspiration before her computer and awakening in the middle of the night, restless with the ache of unfulfilled passion. Suddenly it was as if the door to Ms. Behavior's libido became unhinged, and Ms. Behavior could not close it again. She instantly became a regular on the lesbian chat lines, sitting in front of her overheated computer each night until her eyes grew blurry and her back ached.

In a matter of days, Ms. Behavior found herself in the throes of serious addiction. If forced away from the computer for more than three or four hours at a time, she started to itch and shake. By the time five or six hours had passed, she exhibited symptoms of serious jonesing. Her nose itched, her palms sweated, and her attention span deteriorated. By the eight-hour mark, her body's reaction made her choices clear: Sign on or die.

One night, while six of her friends played poker in her living room, Ms. Behavior kept slipping out of the room to check her e-mail and see who was online. She could not help it; although her mother had raised her to be a polite hostess, she was compelled to enter her office repeatedly, as if it contained a special magnetic force that pulled her in by her fillings. She sat down and typed her password, relieved from the distress of withdrawal only by intimate conversation with Luscious77. The relief that came with Luscious77's slow, sensual, virtual kisses was a warm and instant wave throughout her body; it was like getting a hit of a powerful drug.

By Ms. Behavior's fifth or sixth absence from the living room, her friends noticed her odd disappearances. By the seventh time, they gathered in her office to see what she was doing. By the eighth time, they planned an intervention.

Despite Ms. Behavior's vehement objections and her careful insistence that she was only engaging in social virtual sensuality, her friends unplugged her computer, put a chastity belt around it, and removed it from her house. Ms. Behavior followed them into the street, begging, pleading, wailing, and finally cursing, but they refused to take pity on her. Rita, Ms. Behavior's largest and scariest friend, tucked the computer into the back of her Jeep and refused to let Ms. Behavior near it. Beth, the most sympathetic of the bunch (who perhaps felt responsible for inspiring Ms. Behavior's addiction), put a comforting arm around her and allowed Ms. Behavior to cry on her shoulder.

Then, in a tightly orchestrated circle, they ushered Ms. Behavior back into the house and forced her to begin the detoxification process. They sat in a circle on her floor and lectured her about sexual intimacy and love. They reminded her that being a cyberslut was keeping her at a distance from the people who cared for her the most in a *real* way. Every time she looked as if she might bolt for the door, they held her down firmly (with their feet). Since it was Christmas week and almost everyone was off from work, Ms. Behavior's friends took turns staying with her for eight-hour shifts, thus preventing Ms. Behavior from sneaking out to use someone else's computer. When her physical withdrawal became unbearable, they held ice to her lips and rocked her shivering body against their fleshy bosoms.

After six or seven days, the black circles around Ms. Behavior's eyes started to fade. The color returned to her cheeks, and the ache in her back began to subside. She could envision finding a reason to live again, even without the possibility of communication with Luscious77, Sallylingus, Melonsgalore, and her other cyberpals. Her actual-reality friends slowly began to allow her to return to her normal routine, but only for a few minutes at a time and with careful supervision.

Now that a few months have passed since her forced detoxification, Ms. Behavior understands a lot more about addiction than she ever did before. If anything positive has come out of Ms. Behavior's tireless research, it is this advice that she can offer to her readers: If you suffer from any sort of compulsive tendencies, stay far, far away from virtual sensuality, or the same thing could very well happen to you. One day you are a normal productive human being, and the next day you're the victim of an uncontrollable obsession, compelled from the center of your soul to have long, meaningless conversations with women named after fruit and porn stars.

Ms. Behavior remembers the feeling of desperation that arose from knowing that people were online when she could not be, and the longing and emptiness that that knowledge touched inside her. She remembers thinking, "Just one more time and then I'll stop," and rationalizing that at least she wasn't doing drugs. She also remembers Luscious77 saying, "Please, baby, please," and it still gives her chills up and down her spine.

Chapter Nineteen

✦ ✦ ✦

LESBIANS AND GAY
MEN IN RECOVERY

Hi, your name is Mary, and you're an alcoholic. Oops. Pardon Ms. Behavior. She keeps forgetting that you will have to determine that for yourself. If you take too long deciding, though, others are sure to assist you.

One day you are happily drinking and drugging and occasionally passing out on the bathroom floor, and the next day you are screwing up all over the place. Soon your picky friends and family gang up on you and confront you about your "substance abuse problem." At first you are sure that you can stop anytime you want. "Maybe just one more beer," you say, tossing another one back. Barely even slurring your words, you're certain that you are still the wittiest, liveliest creature in the room.

Perhaps the thing that ultimately disturbs you is not being able to remember who you went home with the night before and what you did. You pretend it doesn't matter, but when all your friends share stories of their safe-but-fun sexual exploits, you cannot participate, because you don't remember whether it was safe and you don't remember whether it was fun.

If you eventually find that you do have a pesky alcohol or drug problem, do not despair. It means that you have the opportunity to join a twelve-step program such as Alcoholics Anonymous or Narcotics Anonymous, and that after a while most of your non-alcoholic friends will be jealous of your huge network of funny, interesting, queer and sober friends. (Some of these will be the same people who used to dance wildly next to you at the clubs, occasionally cavorting naked on the speakers.)

You arrive at AA dazed and bewildered and are told you need to choose a sponsor, someone who can help guide you through the steps of recovery. If you are like most people, you look around the room, see someone cute, and start fantasizing about exactly the kind of guidance you might need. Uh-oh. Ms. Behavior suggests that you stop right there and rule out anyone for whom you have lascivious feelings, or even a quickened heartbeat. It is natural to want loving support from someone you might like to date (or at least boff), but it is actually best if you choose a sponsor whom you find unattractive, someone you would not want to touch even after a decade of forced celibacy. It might be even better to choose someone you *know* you'd never want to touch: someone of the opposite sex.

Why can't you have a beautiful same-sex sponsor? Because her wise and reassuring words of sobriety would be wasted on you; you would be too busy trying to look down her shirt. Or, if you're a man, you'd be staring at that one button on his 501s that never seems to stay closed. Besides, you would not want to tell this person the gory details of your drinking history, because you would obsessively wonder if they might make you unappealing. Each time you were in your sponsor's presence, you would obsess about your hair and your basic worth as a person, which would interfere with deriving anything meaningful out of the meetings you might attend together.

Your sober friends suggest that you stay out of relationships for your first year of sobriety. This sounds harsh, and kind of like a prison term. But meetings, meditation, and masturbation are the suggested forms of entertainment for your first year, because those annoying little emotions that relationships bring to the surface can be a catalyst for relapse. Besides, if you date someone from meetings, this person will be considered a pariah; getting involved with a newcomer, also known as "thirteen-stepping," is regarded as sleazy. (Not that this will prevent certain sharklike people from staring and circling when you first walk in.)

You hear most of what you need to know about sobriety from your sponsor and your sober friends. They give you suggestions for changing your habits so you won't get drunk again. They recommend, for example, that you do not spend all your time hanging out in the places where you drank and drugged, with the same tired old homosexuals who drank and drugged with you. This is good advice, because you might otherwise be tempted to throw your dress on (or off) and kick your heels up on the sound system once again.

There is, however, one thing that your loyal friends do not remember to tell you, an uncomfortable but necessary piece of advice that Ms. Behavior is forced to dispense: *Do not "share" your feelings all over the place.*

Ms. Behavior has seen it happen too many times. You get sober and your feelings rise to the surface like so many blue and bobbing cadavers. You become an excavator of your own soul, poking around, trying to see how deep inside yourself you can go, just for sport. Soon you begin to learn the basics of communication, how to express the feelings that you have been stuffing or numbing with alcohol and drugs for years. Self-examination and self-expression become your favorite activities. The problem, however, is that instead of quietly speaking with your friends or your sponsor, you babble about your feelings to the grocer, the pharmacist, your lover's mother, your eighty-year-old neighbor who has Alzheimer's, your boss, and anyone who is not sensible enough just to scream and run away.

It is difficult to learn not to spill your feelings all over because there is sometimes little support for self-restraint. It partly depends on the group you join, but some pockets of recovering people clearly think it is not only normal but good to have daily crises and weekly explorations of your grossest, blackest feelings. These are sometimes referred to as the "issues and tissues" groups of Alcoholics Anonymous. Such groups are easy to recognize, because the members cry one at a time while the others offer earnest gazes and supportive pats on the back.

Outside of your recovery circle, your social life will suffer if you talk about your feelings all the time. You will be avoided like someone who has found religion. Your friends will no longer invite you to parties. Or, if invited, you will be locked in a basement room with one other sober person and a bottle of club soda, because if allowed to roam freely, you will drink Diet Cokes so fast you'll think you've had a real drink and then talk everyone else into a coma. Even your tolerant lover will get fed up with you and throw things and tell you to shut up. If that doesn't work, he might even get frustrated enough to offer you a beer, just for a few minutes of peace.

A recovering alcoholic who recovers his feelings is a lot like an infant who first finds his genitals; you think you have discovered something new and exciting and you cannot stop playing with it. Luckily, Ms. Behavior is here to remind you that feelings are really everyday occurrences (and so are genitals, for that matter). If you keep this in mind, maybe it will prevent you from babbling about your personal growth during your film class. Perhaps it will save your poor mother from having to tell you every detail of your childhood so that you can "understand where you're coming from." Your lover, too, will appreciate your refraining from endless revelations of your darkest, stickiest emotions and does not need to be dragged into a confessional each day. (Ms. Behavior would also like to remind you that if you must share, you should do it with an ice cream cone, not your feelings.)

The thing about feelings is that some of them are meant to be private. Intimacy is meant to happen with people who welcome your disclosures, not with random strangers on the subway. Whatever happened to shame, anyway? Ms. Behavior urges you to remember that those feelings of shame that you're working so hard to eradicate are really a societal safety net, which is what allows you to be tolerated by people who might otherwise be forced to stomp you into the dust.

Ms. Behavior hopes you understand, because next time she is at a cocktail party and someone starts telling her about all of his embarrassing childhood moments, she will surely laugh out loud and shame him into never "sharing" again. And each time Ms. Behavior does this, she expects to be thanked by the hundreds of people who might otherwise have been forcibly subjected to these very same disclosures.

After a year of sobriety, your life changes. This is partly because you are no longer brand-new and people in recovery stop coddling you. It is also because you are now free to get involved with someone and wreck your life. You have permission to put another person in the position of your higher power, which is often what happens once you have been romance- and sex-free for a year. You might be inclined to do anything this person tells you, because you are so grateful to have the thrill of courtship back in your life. (Bear in mind, though, that dating another person from AA, particularly if she has also been sober for about a year, is like going out with someone from the next ward in your mental institution.)

Once you've been sober for a while, you find out some things you don't want to know. For one thing, the steps are not like the Ten Commandments; you can't just read them once and then forget them. You have to work at them in order to change. This is particularly annoying.

Soon, however, you might realize that you like being sober. You eventually gain a sense of sanity. You make a lot of cool new friends. Perhaps best of all, you remember what you did last night and are able to recall the names of the people you spent time with. Ms. Behavior also suspects it is comforting to be able to remember the details of your exciting sexual experiences, in case you ever want to write a book.

Chapter Twenty

✦ ✦ ✦

CODEPENDENT IF YOU
WANT ME TO BE

ou might be considered fortunate if your lover is smart, funny, or attractive. But if you are lucky enough to find someone who is codependent, be sure to count your blessings every day. (Or get your lover to do it for you.)

Ms. Behavior would now like to extol the virtues of codependency and to warn against encouraging your loved one to "recover" from this supposedly undesirable state. Codependent people care too much how you feel about them and will do anything you want them to do, and even anything they *think* you might want them to do, because they need to be liked and loved. The good thing about codependent people is the very thing that "recovery" attempts to change: They live to please you.

It is Ms. Behavior's contention that if we all had a couple of codependent people in our lives, the world would be a happier place. If each person had someone who lived for the mere pleasure of fetching things and making her happy, wouldn't that reduce the incidence of loneliness and sadness? Wouldn't it diminish the frequency of street crime?

Be honest. Wouldn't you like someone like that in your life right now? So what if this behavior is pathological? If your own special codependent wants to see only the movies you want to see and eat only the food you like and rub your feet at night and call your boss to explain why you are not at work, is this necessarily negative? If it fulfills the codependent's need to fulfill your every need, how bad can that be?

Ms. Behavior has a newfound deep appreciation and love for people who are active codependents. She has noticed that it is only when people enter recovery from codependency that they become truly annoying. Think of this horrifying scenario: Your formerly sweet, eager-to-please lover suddenly begins to consider her needs, to the detriment of yours. One of the first signs of this ugly transition is when she begins to start sentences with "I have a need to tell you that I am feeling . . ." Soon her vocabulary will focus on nine primary words. A typical sentence using each of these words might be "I need to share with you that I feel you are abandoning me, and it makes me feel shame because you can see my vulnerability, and I really need validation from you about my self-worth so that I don't develop a fear of intimacy or inappropriate boundaries."

Ms. Behavior has herself packed boxes late into the night at the first sign of so-called recovery from codependency. Once, after emerging wet and sudsy from a bathtub, she dressed without even drying off as her lover earnestly explained her newfound set of boundaries, which included no hugging without asking and no eating her lactose-free ice cream without permission.

Ms. Behavior hopes you understand the gravity of this. Once your lover discovers his codependency issues, you can forget about spending a relaxing evening at the movies or casually hanging out with friends. Most of your time with the recovering codependent will now be consumed with dissecting feelings, discussing needs, and analyzing trivial aspects of your behavior.

Not only will you have to withstand the torture of therapyspeak, this is the end of life as you have known it. Your formerly easygoing lover is about to go on a self-actualization/freedom-from-codependency kick, and *your* needs, once the focal point of your codependent's universe, are about to be cavalierly tossed aside like so much nonrecyclable rubbish. Having grown used to the joys of codependency, you will not like this new attitude one bit. Imagine how you might feel if after sex he no longer looks into your eyes and says, "*Wow!* That was great for you! How was it for me?" You will find yourself shaking your lover (who has "forgotten" to set his alarm for two hours earlier than he needs to be up so that he can make you coffee) and screaming, "What about *me? Me! Me!! Me!!! HELLO!??*"

Ms. Behavior hates to overwhelm her readers but the truth about this gets even worse. Before the advent of recovery from codependency, if someone's family was nuts, she just said that she came from a fucked-up family. Now there is a whole different language for describing familial insanity. If someone comes from a family that might be accurately described as whacked, bonkers, or just plain gonzo, once in recovery, she will now look down to the floor with wistful eyes and say that she comes from a dysfunctional family. Perhaps Ms. Behavior is too nostalgic, but she longs for the days when fucked-up was just fucked-up.

Recovering codependents are also prone to talking about the dreaded "inner child." Ms. Behavior understands that this concept comes from a misguided attempt to help people who were not appropriately nurtured in childhood — because of being raised in a fucked-up (oops, dysfunctional) home — to reparent themselves. Self-love and self-healing are not bad ideals, but still, this child-within notion comes across as pretty icky. Whining seems to be an intrinsic part of recovery from codependency, especially once that demanding inner child has been released. So far as Ms. Behavior can tell, the inner child is a brat who needs to be sent to bed without dinner. Or perhaps to a good Catholic school.

Ms. Behavior has heard people say that they are buying gifts for their inner children, or that they are taking them to the movies. An acquaintance even told Ms. Behavior that she had taken her kid to

Disney World, and she described the child's reaction to the rides at great length before disclosing that the kid she was referring to was her inner child. If Ms. Behavior had had the power to institutionalize this person, she would have considered it an act of kindness.

When your lover or friends begin to talk about their inner children, you can thank them for sharing at you and then try to change the subject. However, some people are very persistent in this conversation, and if you allow it, they will begin to talk like children and you will have to spend the next decade watching them evolve through a second adolescence. When it reaches this point, the only choice you have is to try to remember cruel things from your childhood and threaten or ridicule them. Ms. Behavior is aware that this might sound mean, but it is actually benevolent. Otherwise, your formerly seminormal friend will soon be playing with dolls and jacks at work, spending all of his free time at Disney movies, and dragging his teddy bear to social functions. (A sure sign of someone early in codependency recovery is the omnipresent bear, who "speaks" in a high-pitched voice, saying things the codependent wishes he could say.)

If things get really bad, you may need to join a support group for people who have lost their lovers to recovery from codependency. Keep in mind that intervention is sometimes necessary, which might mean kidnapping your lover, taking her away from her meetings, and reminding her of how much better you liked her before, when she was expressing her love in a more direct manner, through food and favors. Insist that her devotion to you has changed your life and that "those recovery people" are just brainwashing her and her inner child. Once she seems to be somewhat influenced by your sentiments, withdraw from her. This will initiate the chase cycle. The more you withdraw, the more the codependent will want to sink her hooks back into you. Soon she will be saying things like "If you leave me, can I come with you?"

If all else fails and you lose your lover to recovery, Ms. Behavior would like to remind you that codependents are everywhere, and it won't be hard to find another. An aptly written personal ad will grab you a handful of hungry codependents who can't wait to make you feel better. An appropriate headline for your ad would be "My Feelings — Your Specialty," or "I Just Can't Care for Me Like You Do." Ms. Behavior predicts it will only be a matter of moments before you have a bevy of nice codependents calling, eagerly offering to help you pay for the ad.

Part Four

GAY MEN &
LESBIANS IN A
STRAIGHT
ENVIRONMENT

Chapter Twenty-One

✦ ✦ ✦

STRAIGHT ACTING,
STRAIGHT APPEARING?

There are people who will tell you that it is not polite to act like a queen in public places, but it is Ms. Behavior's firm belief that one should never be polite at the expense of dispensing with one's personality or identity. This means that if you are truly a big old queen at your core, you should not be expected to act like a truck driver just because you go out to the movies or a restaurant. This is not only unnatural but dangerous, because holding your queeny tendencies in can cause you to explode. (And queens don't like stretch marks.)

Five male friends of Ms. Behavior's were recently thrown out of a restaurant for acting "too gay." According to Ms. Behavior's reliable friend Oogie, two of the boys were laughing loudly and snapping their fingers in a wide arc over their heads in imitation of their friend Maurice, a flashy queen who was not there. They also sent back their steaks, which were a little raw; otherwise, Oogie swears, they were all well behaved. But as soon as this joyous group of homosexuals had finished eating their entrées, the manager dropped their check on the table and asked them to leave. He would not even allow them to have coffee.

Oogie felt certain that the only reason they were asked to leave is that they were a noticeable group of somewhat nellyish gay men. In Ms. Behavior's opinion, the only infraction of politeness committed by this group was imitating Maurice in his absence, and even that wasn't so bad, because they've been known to do it in his presence too, to his delight.

The manager's conduct was reprehensible and deserving of retribution. Ms. Behavior felt, when consulted on the matter later, that these lovely gay men should have formed a singing quintet in front of the restaurant and put on a free performance. They all know the words to certain songs, such as "It's Raining Men," "Love to Love You, Baby," "So Many Men, So Little Time," and "I'm Every Woman," and they could have put on a wonderful seventies-style concert, with costumes, smoke, and lights.

Some lesbians confront the same problem when people expect them to behave in a stereotypically "ladylike" manner or to dress in an uncomfortable way. A giant dyke should not, for example, be expected to don a dress and a pair of heels just because she is going to work. This can cause mental and emotional stress, which would interfere with her job performance, and also might look downright silly. What looks funnier than a big, athletic lesbian clomping around in pumps? (Don't say a drag queen!) Some lesbians happen to feel comfortable in dresses, not like they have been forced into some kind of horrible costume, which is fine. Those who are not comfortable, however, should be allowed to wear anything that is nice and reasonably dressy (as long as they have the good judgment not to wear their gladiator outfits to work).

Ms. Behavior first noticed the potential for expectations of total femininity to become a problem in her own life when she was about twelve. The adolescent Ms. Behavior was shoe shopping with her glamorous mother when it became apparent that her glamorous mother was making ugly faces at every shoe Ms. Behavior liked. Ms. Behavior fancied shoes that looked like they had cleats, while her mother expressed an obvious preference for toe-crunching high heels. Not surprisingly, Ms. Behavior's mother has toes that look like crustacean claws. (Sorry, Mom.) So at that tender young age, Ms. Behavior was forced to choose between wearing hideous shoes that made her feel as if she were dressed in costume and risking her mother's disapproval. Guess which she chose?

Now that she is old enough to choose her shoes without parental intervention, Ms. Behavior has an affinity for big clunky flats and Birkenstocks, which her straight friends refer to as her Fred Flintstone shoes. Unlike some of her more culturally assimilated lesbian friends, Ms. Behavior refuses to wear shoes that are even mildly uncomfortable, not even to a funeral or a job interview, or both, as the case may sometimes be. She believes in the fundamental liberty to have uncrippled toes, and would lobby endlessly for the right to comfortable footwear. It is almost a fetish with her. This is her platform!

If Ms. Behavior's mother had known that her disdain for her twelve-year-old child's footwear would cause a permanent lesbian shoe fixation, she probably would have altered her behavior. But alas, it is now too late.

If you understand the basic concept that it is okay to be yourself, but you think you might need frequent reinforcement, get a hold of Marlo Thomas's old album *Free to Be You and Me*. Play it every day. Dance around your apartment, wearing your most comfortable shoes, kicking your imaginary enemies in the head, and letting the lyrics fill your mind. After a month or so of grooving to these tunes on a daily basis, write to Ms. Behavior and let her know how you feel.

Chapter Twenty-Two

✦ ✦ ✦

COMING OUT TO YOUR PARENTS

*N*ever mind the silly advice books on coming out to your parents, which are filled with wimpy suggestions; Ms. Behavior thinks it is usually best just to blurt it out in ordinary conversation. Invite them to your house for dinner and serve dessert as you watch the news together. Wait for a semirelevant moment and then say, "Mom, Dad, as a lesbian/gay man [pick whichever applies], I am truly appalled at what the Republicans are doing to this country." Then ask them to pass the tiramisu and see what happens.

If your parents quietly pass the dessert, you will know that they are sunk so deep into denial as to be rendered deaf. You could stand on the coffee table and say "I love to lick boys" (or girls, as the case may be), and they would continue to talk about the weather, the stock market, or the price of Hefty bags (which reflects an unconscious desire to kill you and stuff you into one). Your parents just do not want to know, so no amount of serious proclaiming or chest-beating will make them hear you at this point. You are the tree that has fallen in an unoccupied forest. You are the hand clapping alone.

If your parents are like this, you will soon realize that they have ignored nearly every important thing you have ever told them, and you will spend at least three years in therapy discussing how your invisibility within your family has affected your life. As you get in touch with your anger about this, you may find yourself compelled to shave and dye a pink triangle on the back of your head, or you will become obsessed with trying to arrange an appearance on *Oprah*, with the caption "Invisible Carpet Muncher" beneath your face.

Some parents have very noisy and dramatic responses to the coming-out thang. Just think of their explosive reaction as a scary thunderstorm, which will pass. When Ms. Behavior's friend George came out to his parents, his father, Herb, fell to his knees, clutched his chest, and began to curse. "Oh God, take me now," he screamed. "My son is a cocksucker! He's a fudgepacker! He takes it up the ass!" George was put off by this outburst and went out to buy himself some ice cream for a little binge. By the time he returned home with several pints of Häagen-Dazs, his father was sitting in his chair drinking tea, as if he had not just been crawling around George's kitchen floor on his knees. Once Herb was done with his initial blaring reaction, he went back to his usual mild-mannered demeanor and joined his son for some Mocha Almond Fudgepacker.

Ms. Behavior is here to remind you that even if your parents yell and throw tantrums and threaten to disown you, they usually don't mean it. They may think they mean it at the time, and they may truly be upset, but ultimately they will probably come to their senses and realize that they still want to keep you in the family, despite your odd emotional and sexual proclivities. Parents who detonate upon hearing the news frequently become the ones who call all their friends to remind them to watch the television program about how homosexuality is genetically determined and who keep gay-related "Dear Abby" clippings hanging from little pizza-shaped magnets on their refrigerators.

If your parents try to send you to a shrink in the hope of converting you, you can gently remind them that their money would be better spent on psychotherapy for themselves (or Valium), which might allow them to get to a more peaceful, accepting place. Nearly any right-minded psychotherapist would be likely to approach the issue from this point of view anyway. (Of course, your parents could luck out and find some kind of sadistic weirdo who might actually want to try to give you electric shocks in conjunction with same-sex erotic stimulation, à la *Clockwork Orange*.)

The only time you should worry is when your parents seem very warm and accepting when you come out to them. This is a sure sign of major misery ahead. If your coming-out is met with love, approval, and support, you should (a) worry, (b) seek psychiatric support, and (c) run. This sort of aberrant reaction generally means that your parents are either suppressing their true feelings of shock and rage, which will slowly leak out like a toxic poison over time, or sincere in their support and will soon embarrass you by appearing on national television carrying signs saying "I love my queer son" or "My daughter is a lezzie and I am proud."

Soon your parents' station wagon will be covered with rainbow flags and bumper stickers. Every time you go out shopping, you will find your parents hanging out in front of Foodtown, handing out leaflets in support of gay and lesbian rights. The next thing you know, your father will be marching next to you during Gay Pride, wearing a dress and a pair of cheap size 14 pumps. You will never again be able to march with just your friends without hurting your tag-along father's feelings. (And he looks so pathetic crying in that dress.) Your mother will get a crew cut in solidarity with the transgendered, and you will see her on the six o'clock news, sporting a new five o'clock shadow, protesting about having been kicked out of the PTA. Some of your friends will think your parents are immensely cool, but you will be mortified beyond belief and will lie awake at night yelling at God for not giving you normal, rejecting parents who would cross you out of the will.

Ms. Behavior has known some people who have had to pretend to be straight just to stop their parents from being excessively supportive. Ms. Behavior's friend the Trouser Trout had a horrifying coming-out experience. His parents, Flo and Myron, joined P-FLAG (Parents and Friends of Lesbians and Gays) the minute he came out to them as a teenager. In fact, they ran for the telephone to call P-FLAG before he had even finished saying the word "gay." Soon Myron was president of the local P-FLAG chapter and appearing on *Good Morning, America* with regularity. He also forced the Trout to appear on television shows with a caption beneath his face that said "Gay Teenager," until the Trout's guidance counselor took pity on him and mercifully begged Myron to stop booking these engagements. The Trout spent the next six months pretending to be interested in girls, out of fear that his parents would resume their supportive behavior.

Ms. Behavior firmly believes that coming out should always be done either on your own turf or on neutral territory. You do not, for example, want to come out in the living room of the house you grew up in, the place where your parents changed your diapers and wiped up your spilled apple juice. You especially do not want to sit on the edge of the trundle bed in your old bedroom and tell them that you're gay; the power imbalance will be too great, and you will start talking in a high, childish voice. Also, if your parents do end up having a fit, you might need to be able to quietly and dramatically ask them to leave, which is difficult to do in their home.

Regardless of which kind of parents you have, when you are finished coming out you will need two things: (a) something with which to stuff your feelings, and (b) the support of your friends. The best way to combine these things is to go out with your friends on some kind of feeding frenzy the minute you have come out. The more you eat, the better you will feel. A full stomach will make you unable to determine which of your nauseous feelings are emotional in origin. It will also give you that stuffed sensation, which will make you less conscious of your feelings generally, a power that should never be underrated. Also, if you end up vomiting later as a reaction to the whole experience, you can always blame it on the fried clams, beer, burgers, and ice cream.

Chapter Twenty-Three

✦ ✦ ✦

"STRAIGHTENING UP"
YOUR APARTMENT
FOR VISITORS

*M*s. Behavior's family is nosy. When they first came to visit her at college, they poked around her dorm room, touching mugs with double woman signs and labryses. Soon they were in fierce clue-gathering mode, snooping around the room with their tongues hanging out like a bunch of drug-sniffing dogs. Once they had scrutinized the college-era bumper stickers and buttons with slogans like "Don't Die Wondering," their collective gaze fell upon the prints taped to the walls, which were of naked women in various poses. Ms. Behavior could practically hear them wondering, is this just art, or is it an unnatural preoccupation with female bodies? She was prepared to tell them that it was both, if they asked, but they didn't.

Ms. Behavior has now been out to her family for well over a decade, and she does not bother straightening up at all when they visit. She realizes that it wouldn't actually matter what she left lying around her apartment; they have become too nervous to look closely at anything she might own.

Some people feel squeamish about leaving their lives open to the view of straight family members and other visitors, even once they are out. Such people often say things like "It is one thing to be out. It is another to leave evidence of your deviance strewn all around your apartment when you have company."

Ms. Behavior's response to such an attitude can be summarized in five words: Don't be such a wuss. She would always support your decision to leave your possessions as they are, in a way that reflects the life you live. Your framed print from last year's Gay Pride march reflects something about where you've been and what is important to you. Your colorful, labial Georgia O'Keeffe prints should remain too, in a deeply patriotic visual display of the glorification of both flowers and vaginas. And boys, there is really no reason to remove that lovely, vibrant picture of the rooster that says "Gay Cock."

Ms. Behavior's friend Jake used to hide his drag wigs and replace all of his Barbra Streisand albums with U2 music when he had visitors. Now that he has evolved to a point of self-acceptance, he turns up the volume on his homo tunes and leaves photos of himself dressed as Joan Rivers scattered all around the apartment.

There are a few exceptions to Ms. Behavior's conviction about leaving things as they are. It might be prudent, for example, to remove your tattered copies of *Honcho* or *On Our Backs* from your coffee table, so that your mother does not faint. (Actually, straight people are not the only ones in danger of passing out; some of the pierced-labia photos in *On Our Backs* have caused the otherwise resilient Ms. Behavior nearly to lose consciousness, too.) And although it is most likely not *you* posing in these magazines, there is something icky about revealing even an appreciation for explicit sexuality to your parents.

If you happen to be among those people who view sex toys as art and leave them sitting proudly erect on your coffee table, you might want to consider stowing them in a drawer until your family leaves. This suggestion also applies to the whips and handcuffs you have hanging from your ceiling, never mind that big studded leather harness and the Pleasure Swing. Dildos, vibrators, and other phallically inclined apparatus generally push even the mellowest of parents over the edge into hysteria (with the possible exception of the mother of Ms. Behavior's friend Francesca, who gave each of her daughters a huge and effective "massager" for Christmas). If, however, you have those nonrepresentational dildos that look like dolphins or hat-wearing men with woodchucks on their shoulders, you can probably get away with leaving them sitting chastely around your living room. (But the obsessively hygienic Ms. Behavior recommends doing so only if you have washed them thoroughly.)

When family members or other folks come to visit, they also have the opportunity to see your apartment layout and to ask you questions based on their observations. Ms. Behavior's friend Tommy-Tuna had never explicitly come out to his Aunt Tillie, but he assumed she knew he was gay because he had lived with his lover, Steve, for years. When Tommy-Tuna gave Aunt Tillie a tour of their new home, she asked, upon seeing only one bedroom, "Where does Steve sleep?" Tommy pointed to the bed and said, "On the left." Ms. Behavior admired Tommy's response, because he both came out and normalized the situation in one fell swoop, effectively fielding and scoring with just a short phrase.

The straightening-up issue extends beyond the realm of aesthetics into the area of behavior. Like, will you and your lover sit on opposite ends of the couch, avoiding physical contact, or will you feel free to squeeze his hand occasionally or tousle his hair?

Ms. Behavior has never enjoyed watching people swap spit or grope, and she thinks such behavior is rude in public or even when you have company at home. No one likes to see that little strand of saliva that you think is so cute hanging from your lover's lips. But small, affectionate gestures are perfectly sweet, and whoever doesn't like them can suck rocks.

If you are ever forced to actually live with straight friends or family members, compromises (not to mention prayers) are sometimes necessary to maintain comfort (not to mention sanity). After having numerous brawls about both aesthetics and politics, Ms. Behavior's forty-year-old friend Laura finally came to an agreement with her teenage daughter, Woolf, about what sorts of things each would be permitted to hang on the walls of their shared apartment. Ultimately, Woolf had to agree to give up the poster of Marky Mark in his underwear in exchange for Laura's removal of the poster that showed one woman going down on another, with a caption that said "Power Breakfast."

Ms. Behavior believes this to be a perfect example of the willingness to compromise and coexist in delightful harmony. If only our world leaders would adopt such negotiation strategies, the planet would spin on its axis in peaceful and unified bliss. No more strife, no more crime, no more food shortages, no more bad hair. Meditate on such gentle images each morning, and the world will be a better place in time for the new millennium.

✦ ✦ ✦

Dear Ms. Behavior:

I'm a gay man and have been comfortably out to my friends, family, and coworkers for a long time. I'm writing because recently my father came over to my house completely dressed in leather and came out to me and all my friends. Since then, he makes a habit of telling me about his twenty-three-year-old stud-muffin conquests, which makes me queasy. Ms. Behavior, while I love and accept my father for who he is and I respect and honor his process of self-discovery, I am ashamed to tell you that frankly, I am repulsed by the whole thing. I am kept awake nights, horrified by visions of Dad in compromising positions. I live in terror of running into him at a bar and seeing him fawning over one of my old friends from high school. It's not fair. I shouldn't have to deal with this. Ms. Behavior, what can I do?

— Skeeved

Dear Skeeved:

Your father's homosexuality is beautiful. Do not come along with your big sharp knife and snip the flower of his emergent sexual expression in the bud. If it grosses you out to envision your daddy with his legs in the air, then don't!

Your reaction, however, is normal. You are supposed to be utterly nauseated by the thought of either of your parents gasping and wailing in orgasmic pleasure. But entertaining such thoughts and allowing them to linger is clearly a misuse of your Goddess-given imagination. Ms. Behavior suggests you train your mind to stop engaging in this sort of envisioning immediately, or you will surely implode.

Ms. Behavior also predicts that five years from now, you and your father will be scouring the bars together in pursuit of hot young stud muffins. She only hopes that you and your daddy don't have the same taste.

Chapter Twenty-Four

✦ ✦ ✦

WHAT TO DO IF YOU ARE INVITED TO A WEDDING OR FORMAL EVENT WITHOUT YOUR LOVER

Over the past decade, Ms. Behavior has happily declined every invitation to every formal event that has not included the phrase "and guest." Ms. Behavior prefers to think that this is not a codependency issue. It's just that traditional weddings are bad enough *with* a date; attending them alone is an unreasonable torture that no right-minded homosexual should be forced to endure. Besides the usual wedding offenses, such as orchestral music, bad food, and drunken, overbearing relatives who badger you about when *you* are getting married, the homophobic omission of the person you love (or like a lot) should at least evoke some righteous indignation.

So how do you decide whether or not to attend a formal event if you are invited without a date? Well, if this happens during a time that you happen to be single, the ugly reality might be one you can deal with, particularly if the heterosexual attendees were not invited to bring guests either. (Of course, it takes tact and good research skills to extract this information in a subtle way, but Ms. Behavior trusts that you can do so.) And while it would have been far more gracious for the host to have extended an invitation to bring a guest whether or not you have a lover, one cannot always afford to be gracious. Such an "oversight" when you are single might be considered excusable.

If, however, you have a lover and are invited without him or her, you need to assess your relationship with the people who have invited you. It generally means one of the following things: (a) They don't know you have a lover; (b) They know you have a lover but were stricken with amnesia and "forgot" when they were sending out the invitations; (c) They judge your relationship with your lover as less than meaningful; (d) They know you have a lover but are too cheap to invite him or her; (e) They are afraid you will create a big queer scene by pressing your bodies together on the dance floor; (f) They fear that you and your lover might have loud, uncontrollable sex in the bathroom or touch tongues at the table and cause the other guests to run screaming into the parking lot, taking their gifts; (g) They don't want you both groping for the bouquet.

The first thing you must do when you get the guest-free invitation to the dreaded event is to try to figure out which category the host's or hostess's ignorance falls into (unless you are so annoyed by the matter that you just automatically decline, which is also okay). Invitation in hand, you call the person who has invited you. The conversation might go something like this:

Ms. BEHAVIOR: Hi, Aunt Ethel. Congratulations on your impending marriage. And thank you for your invitation.

AUNT ETHEL: Blah blah blah.

Ms. BEHAVIOR: Oh yes, the family is fine. And Zoe and I have just celebrated our fourth anniversary. You met Zoe, right? Yes, she is doing very well.

AUNT ETHEL: Blah blah blah.

MS. BEHAVIOR: The funny thing is, I seem to have misplaced the invitation. I think it said I was invited with a guest, yes?

Now here's the tricky part. If Aunt Ethel is a sensible woman and saves face by responding that yes, the invitation was certainly extended to Zoe too, Ms. Behavior's response is one of sweetness and light:

MS. BEHAVIOR: Yes, we would both love to attend. I guess I must have misplaced the reply card with the invitation, but you can check us both off as coming. We are very happy for your lovely union and wish you many years of bliss.

If Aunt Ethel says no, your filthy lesbian lover was not invited, or even if she says no, we were only able to afford to invite the *married* attendees to bring guests, the appropriate response is as follows:

MS. BEHAVIOR: Well, unfortunately, I won't be able to attend your celebration of heterosexual bondage. I do not attend such glorifications of the patriarchy unless I am invited with Zoe, my life partner, and even then I am in danger of retching. So while you and all of your unattractive, mouth-breathing relatives are doing the hora and exchanging mutual approval for your dull lifestyle, Zoe and I will be at home, naked on the floor, rubbing our warm and sweaty bodies together, tribadizing like nobody's business.

Then hang up.

Ms. Behavior would like to believe that if enough gay men and lesbians respond in this manner to insulting invitations, it will eventually effect a change. (No one can predict on a personal level, however, whether the change would be toward including guests in your invitation in the future or just not inviting you anywhere anymore.) The desire by some straight people to be perceived as cool and accepting is spreading, and will work to the queer advantage. In any case, even if there are numerous people who refuse to be relieved of their ignorance, responding to them in this way feels very satisfying.

Now let's say the invitation is properly executed and you do decide to attend a heterosexual union with your lover. If you are a woman, always remember this bit of advice from Ms. Behavior: *No matter what, do not agree to be a bridesmaid.* (If you're a man, the decision is up to you.) First of all, you may not get to sit next to your lover; bridesmaids are often clumped together, dateless, at one big table. Second, *nothing* looks sillier than a giant lesbian in one of those purple taffeta dresses and dyed-to-match pumps. You will spend the whole wedding wishing you could die or just be absorbed into the atmosphere. You will find yourself staring miserably at your shoes, gazing longingly at the exit, praying for a flood or a fire, anything that would allow you to go home and change. You might even go so far as to carelessly empty an ashtray full of burning embers into a trashcan filled with paper.

Ms. Behavior does not mean to imply that you should wear your favorite motorcycle jacket and a pair of jeans; however, an attractive but comfortable middle ground is easy to achieve (and if you need reassurance about your butchness, you can always slip into the bathroom, sneak a peek at your tattoos, and give your nipple ring a tweak).

The clothing issue is more important than you might guess. If you are careful not to dress like the other "girls" (and this holds true for male wedding attendees too), some subtle difference is conveyed in your clothing and demeanor, and people are less apt to ask you stupid and awkward questions about your own life and when *you* might be getting married.

If this happens to be a family wedding to which your mother is also invited, it is crucial to try to avoid sitting next to her. You might even go so far as to switch tables with someone; if that's not feasible, consider sitting under the table. If you and your mother sit together, nosy relatives will definitely ask questions about your prospects for conjugal bliss, and your mother might feel compelled to say something hopeful. You will quickly boil over in response to your mother's optimistic comments and your face will turn red. You will jump up onto the table and scream that you have already met the right person — can't she see your lover standing right there next to you? Then you will grab the microphone from the bandleader and yell about homophobia and about how the hostess didn't initially invite your lover and about how you cannot legally get married so why should you support this ridiculous display of heterosexual commitment anyway? A crowd of people will gather around, each of them holding little pigs in blankets and staring. And you will forever be known as the person who ruined Myra Plotnick's wedding, and will never be invited to another wedding again.

In which case it might all be worth it.

Chapter Twenty-Five

✦ ✦ ✦

WHAT DO YOU CALL

YOUR LOVER?

*H*ey, Pookey-lips, if Ms. Behavior were to recite the entire list of affectionate nicknames you call your lover, you would be embarrassed. You might think she had been hiding under your bed with all the big furry dustballs, spying on you. Luckily for you, though, Ms. Behavior is very allergic to dust and would not be likely to assume that position.

Ms. Behavior is referring to the sugary names that you and your lover call each other in those tender and private moments when you are lying side by side gazing into each other's dilated pupils. Or sometimes you say them absentmindedly as you prepare dinner or rub each other's feet while watching TV. But it's usually when the two of you are alone, isn't it, Pumpkin? You try not to lapse into this sort of sentimental sweetness when other people are around, because it makes you feel immensely uncool.

'Fess up, Sunshine. You call your lover Puddin', Sticky Buns, and Sweet Pea. Ms. Behavior has actually heard you say Muffin, Sweetmeat, Sugar Pie, Cupcake, Lollipop, and Marshmallow Fluff. Your list of edible names is endless and endearing, because those names indicate that you just want to ingest your lover whole, eat him up.

In public you resort to more conventional terms of affection, like Honey, Sweetheart, and Baby, but that's only because others might laugh at you if they heard you call your girlfriend Sweet Potato or Sugar Snap or Potato Chip or Sugar Head. You also might say Honey or Dear when you are pissed off, as in "Honey, how many times do I have to remind you to take out the oozy, smelly bag of garbage that is dripping all over the kitchen floor?" or "Dear, you promised we would only stay at your mother's house for an hour, and it's already been seventeen."

The real difficulty, though, can be deciding how to refer to your lover in his or her absence when talking with straight acquaintances. You are not likely to want to say, "No, I cannot work late tonight, because Sweet Pea and I are going to a concert." And if you just use Sweet Pea's real name, the other person will ask, "Who's that?" which brings you back to the eternal difficulty of finding a word that will describe your relationship.

Some people use the word "lover" under all circumstances, business, social, or otherwise. It is simple, and leaves no doubt in anyone's mind that you are referring to an intimate partner. The problem with the universal usage of that word is that it implies to some straight people that your relationship consists primarily of sex, which they find quite titillating. You utter the word "lover," and the first thing they do is mentally undress you, and then their undisciplined minds propel you into the sack, where they envision you sweating and dripping, making passionate love with Julia Roberts (even if your lover looks more like Gumby). You can be talking about baseball or the weather, and they end up saying something stupid, like "Mmmmmm, faster" so that you know exactly what they have been picturing, and they know that you know.

The word "partner" is less than satisfying for precisely the same reasons that it makes straight people feel comfortable. It is short and businesslike and does not conjure up images of any of that exciting stuff that goes along with more evocative words. If you tell your mother that you have a new partner, she will envision something austere and asexual and may still hold out hope that you will wake up one day and realize that this has all been just a phase. If you refer to Sweet Pea as your partner when you're at work, people will think you mean a business partner and you are moonlighting. Acquaintances will think you are talking about a square-dancing partner or an investment partner or just won't have a clue what the hell you are talking about.

Sweet Pea won't like being referred to as a partner either, because it sounds less than romantic, and she wants to be called only by names that reflect the passion she ignites in you. And if you continue to call her your partner despite her repeated protests, she will stop putting out.

For gay men, the word "boyfriend" is fairly clear in its meaning, but for women, "girlfriend" is not. When women say "girlfriend," most straight people envision Mary and Rhoda or Betty and Wilma, or even Barbie and Midge, and won't think beyond that sort of neighborly or sorority-girl image of women giggling and sharing makeup tips and boy-advice. In some instances it might not be worth your breath to try to distinguish when "girlfriend" means something more, but in other cases, when people seem particularly stubborn in their ignorance, you will be tempted to enlighten them in the most direct way possible. In other words, five minutes of blank staring after your best attempts at explanation may cause you finally to say, "I go down on her. Now do you get it?"

Ms. Behavior has sometimes used the word "paramour" to refer to her lover, but she finds that people either look at her vacantly or assume she is having an affair with a married man. If you choose this word, you will find it particularly disconcerting when people ask you how to spell it.

So what's left? The word "mate" sounds like Noah's Ark, a ship buddy, or a petting zoo. "Main squeeze" is too seventies. "Spouse" is the right idea, but it's an ugly word. "Sweetheart" is quaint. On the homophobic end of the continuum, we still have "roommate." "Other half" is pathetically codependent. After a moment or two of pained staring, "husband" or "wife" usually works in terms of comprehension, but still, it's a little too conventional.

Ms. Behavior expected to offer you a solution in this chapter, but writing it has caused her to realize that there are no suitable choices. She proposes an entirely new language to refer to gay and lesbian coupledom. If each of her readers could submit a suggestion or two, she will be happy to print some alternatives in her next book. Until then, she suggests that you stick to the phrase "hunk of burning love" when referring to that person who sleeps in your bed.

Chapter Twenty-Six

✦ ✦ ✦

DUH! CAN YOU REPEAT THAT STUPID QUESTION??

*W*hile Ms. Behavior is one of this century's greatest proponents of civility and politeness, she has noticed that many lesbians and gay men still spend far too much of their time explaining themselves to straight acquaintances. Some straight people ask a series of Stupid Questions, masquerading their morbid curiosity as an attempt to achieve enlightenment. Ms. Behavior believes that after a brief polite period, you should punish them for Stupid Questions, or at least acknowledge those dopey inquiries for what they are.

If you find yourself placed in this unfortunate position, Ms. Behavior advises you to view them as a cry for help. You may, however, rely on your own capacity to judge when enough is enough. Once you've answered a couple of borderline Stupid Questions, do not allow the conversation to progress into a moron-a-thon.

Some Stupid Questions reflect the underlying assumption that something has gone wrong in your life, which has resulted in your "turning" gay or lesbian. Do not neglect to realize that this is insulting. It all becomes much easier when you remember that such questions can deftly be turned around. For this technique to be effective, you must practice the look of horror you will muster while you ask your inquisitor, "Eeeewwww. When did you turn straight?" and "Really? Do you have any brothers or sisters who are straight too?"

When you do decide to respond to Stupid Questions, the appropriate answer to the ignorant query "When did you turn gay?" is "I didn't know for sure until the beginning of this conversation." Likewise, the "Did you have an overbearing mother?" question can be answered with "I don't know. I'll call her and she'll tell me" or "I was just thinking about how if our mothers were to arm-wrestle, your mother and her overdeveloped biceps would kick my mother's ass."

Questions about your relationship are particularly nosy, but some people ask anyway, as if you are some sort of exotic breed on *Wild Kingdom.* One of Ms. Behavior's favorite questions is "Which one of you is the man?," alternatively expressed as "Who plays the woman?" or "Who's the pitcher?"

Do not be tempted to dignify these inquiries with a serious response. If you are a man and are noticeably more feminine than your partner, the only appropriate reaction is for you to lift your inquisitor a couple of feet off the ground by the front of his shirt and growl, "Who do you think?" If you are noticeably more butch, you may sweetly kiss his hand and then drop to the ground, throwing your legs over your head invitingly.

Feel free at this point to ask your inquisitor questions about his sexual habits. If you really want to see him squirm, ask if he has ever had that spectacular orgasm that can happen only with the prostate stimulation that accompanies anal penetration.

"What do you do in bed?" is primarily asked of lesbians, because while two penises might be considered a liability in the sack, zero penises are considered an unimaginable deficiency. (For some lesbians, this question brings to mind the old 7-Up tag line, "Never had it, never will." Lesbians who have never done it with men are part of an elite club, lesbian lifers.) If you're in a generous mood, you may offer to provide a lezzie sex demonstration, for which you might kindly propose to charge the discounted rate of a quarter. (Of course, if your offer is accepted, you'll have to round up the two biggest, scariest babes you know for the actual exhibition.)

One friend of Ms. Behavior's tells most people who ask, especially her mother, that all she and her lover do in bed is hold hands. No one believes her, and they seem to find this notion deeply disturbing, because it makes them try even harder to picture the vivid truth.

If you use any battery-operated sex toys, you might want to whip them out and turn them on and let them spin around on your coffee table. Stay out of the path to your door, however, or you might get trampled as your guest runs screaming toward the street. (Make sure the toys remain in the house.)

Some of the most irritating questions and assumptions from straight people pertain to HIV and AIDS. Ms. Behavior's friend Oogie left work early one day to attend a memorial service for a friend. A coworker came over to his desk and said, "Wow, another memorial service. Didn't you just have one of those last year?" Oogie quietly crushed his pencil between his fingers and said, "Perhaps you haven't heard this from beneath your particular rock. We are in the midst of an epidemic."

Ms. Behavior recently heard an argument at a nearby table in a restaurant about whether HIV could be transmitted by a chef. One woman knew that food handling was not a risk. The other woman, who insisted that eating food prepared by an HIV-positive chef might be dangerous, thought for a minute and then said, "Well, what if he decided to ejaculate on the salad?" Now here's something Ms. Behavior really wants to know: What kind of sick person would even *think* of such a thing?

Paranoid questions are probably the most fun to field, because at least you have an opportunity for revenge. When a new acquaintance looks at you nervously, mumbles something about accepting your lifestyle, and follows that with "But you know I'm straight, don't you?" never answer affirmatively. Look at her with great seriousness and concern and say, "I knew you were struggling with your sexuality, but I didn't realize how mixed up you were. That must be difficult for you." Pat her on the head for extra support, and run your fingers through her hair while you're at it.

And if you're a man and a straight friend looks at you oddly and says, "You're not making a pass at me, are you?" reassure him that you understand how confusing it can be when homosexual feelings first emerge. Then plant your hand firmly on his knee and tell him with the utmost sincerity that you will always be there for him if he needs to talk about it. Especially if it's late at night.

Chapter Twenty-Seven

✦ ✦ ✦

FRIENDS OF DOROTHY: SNIFFING EACH OTHER OUT IN THE STRAIGHT WORLD

*M*s. Behavior's mother, whom she calls Bubbles, is amazed by gaydar.

It is a Wednesday afternoon, and Bubbles and Ms. Behavior are in the dressing room at Macy's. Ms. Behavior has just made eye contact with a goddesslike lesbian with Pre-Raphaelite hair. Ms. Behavior tries on a loose-fitting, eggshell-colored silk top and emerges from the dressing room to look in the mirror. The goddess approaches, tosses her hair back, and touches Ms. Behavior's shoulder. "That blouse looks fabulous on you. You are very lovely," she says. Ms. Behavior demurely thanks her and quietly imagines how all of that stunning auburn hair might look spread out across her own naked body. Still, she feels weird because her mother is nearby, so she knows she will have to return on another Wednesday to try to find the goddess again.

Ms. Behavior goes back to the dressing room smiling. Bubbles, who has been peeking, is baffled. "How do you gay people always seem to recognize each other?" she whispers. "Is it a secret code or something? A special handshake?" Ms. Behavior just grins mysteriously and allows her mother to wonder. (After all, as a small child she asked her mother to tell her about sex, and it was years before her mother finally relented.)

Bubbles's curiosity about gaydar increased significantly a few years back, after her friend Dotty invited both Bubbles and Ms. Behavior to dinner. The moment Ms. Behavior saw Sabrina, Dotty's daughter, at the dinner table, a wave of sapphic recognition coursed through her, and she knew she was among her own species. Before the appetizers had been finished, Ms. Behavior and Sabrina were discussing *Desert Hearts, Beebo Brinker,* and alternative insemination, as Bubbles and Dotty shoved fruit cup into their mouths and stared in silent astonishment.

Straight people desperately seek concrete answers to how you can tell when someone is gay or lesbian. They want to know if the information lies in something the person wears or does, whether it's a visual clue or a personality characteristic. Why are they so interested in being able to tell? Motives vary; sometimes it is pure curiosity, sometimes the need to feel cool. And for some poor souls it might even be protection against pursuing a relationship with someone who will never be available.

No one has ever expressed a more urgent need for this information than Ms. Behavior's straight friend Thomas, who has a long history of falling in love with women who turn out to be lesbians. "Isn't there some clue, some mannerism I can watch for?" Thomas laments, holding his head. Ms. Behavior just shrugs, although she understands his torment. She wishes she could say that she fell for a woman who ultimately decided she was straight only once, although she is fortunate that it hasn't happened since she was young and inexperienced. So Ms. Behavior admits that it is not only straight people who might benefit from clear ways of detecting whether or not someone is truly gay, but also those who are newly coming out.

For those novices to gay and lesbian life who are still struggling to discern gay men and lesbians from the masses, bear in mind that the clues really are subtle sometimes. It might be something about the way a person looks at you, a gesture you recognize, a similar sensibility, or a T-shirt that says "Let go of my ears. I know what I'm doing." Once you catch on, you will never lose your ability to know. You will feel powerful. Straight people will envy your vision, that special kind of insight that allows you to spot a fag or a dyke from across the room. They will barrage you with questions about how you can tell.

Still, if you meet someone in a mostly straight context, like at work or at a nongay event, there will always be a few instances in which even the most highly developed gaydar doesn't work. Despite your best attempts to tell yourself it doesn't matter, who cares whether your coworker is gay or not, it drives you crazy not to know.

If you are brave, you can try the direct or semidirect verbal method. This involves either asking the person outright if he or she is gay or asking about easily recognizable bars and cultural events. For example, "Hey Harry, didn't I see you at the Ramrod last week? You looked so manly in those chaps." Or, more subtly, "Leslie, did you see the movie *The Hunger?* Wasn't the lesbian seduction scene hot?" There are risks with this method, however. The person you're asking might be embarrassed or caught off guard and pretend not to know what you are talking about, even if he is a regular at the Ramrod or even if she saw the movie eleven times; the person might be gay but oblivious, living in a cultural and social vacuum; or the person might be of that new heterosexual breed of homo wannabes.

For gay men who need to know, it is easy to lapse into a Bette Davis imitation or to recite lines from *Whatever Happened to Baby Jane?* If you call the suspected Nellie "Blanche" and he laughs or quotes along with you, you can be sure he's a poofter. If not, he is either a straight man or a fag with no sense of cultural identity, which is a very sad thing.

Ms. Behavior has heard some people phrase their questions quite delicately. One friend of hers has been known to ask cute men if they are "members of [his] church." Another friend asks people he meets if they are "friends of Dorothy's." The latter idea seems better, because it is less likely to be missed by men who happen to be atheists, Jewish, or Wiccan. Less delicate homosexuals inquire as to whether or not the person in question is "a sistah."

Ms. Behavior is not skilled with such subtlety herself, and is prone to inquiry of a blunter nature. Once when she was in a motorcycle shop helping a friend pick a Honda, she spotted a very attractive woman testing out a motorcycle. The woman was either a cute dyke or a very tough straight biker chick, and Ms. Behavior could not be sure which. Still, she took a risk. "You look great on that bike," Ms. Behavior said, "and I am sure I will now have endless fantasies about holding you from behind while you rev that engine." Before the biker had a chance to respond, Ms. Behavior asked if she planned to ride with the Dykes on Bikes in the next Gay Pride march. Well, since Ms. Behavior still has all her own teeth, you can guess that the biker was in fact a lesbian. She did, however, pause long enough to make fear (and breakfast) rise in Ms. Behavior's stomach, but then she gave her a wide smile and her phone number.

Ms. Behavior's friend Penelope says that she trusts the power of her imagination to tell her if someone is a lesbian or gay. First, with women, she tries to envision them marching in the parade, wearing a sticker that says "Vaginal Pride." If she cannot imagine that, she moves them on to the next test: envisioning them in bed with a man. If she cannot imagine that either, then the litmus test is her final fantasy: imagining them in bed with her. If it seems natural and easy to Penelope, she declares them lesbians.

For men, Penelope runs a similar test. First she imagines them playing baseball. If she can only imagine them throwing like a girl, she then tries to imagine them in bed with a woman. If they fail that test in her mind, she envisions them in bed with Richard Gere. If that works, she declares them gay.

While Ms. Behavior is generally a peaceful and law-abiding citizen, she will admit that in some circumstances of long-standing curiosity, guerrilla tactics have to be introduced. For example, if you're at work and you have tried all of the guessing and asking you can muster and you still have gotten nowhere, it helps if you sit close enough to peek at the contents of the person's gym bag. Although Ms. Behavior is very respectful of privacy, she understands that curiosity can be a painful, nagging sickness, an obsessive ache that can nearly kill you. It is with sensitivity to this anguish that Ms. Behavior would allow you, in instances in which you *must* know someone's sexual orientation and have sincerely tried all other methods, to sneak a glance into the bag. (Do *not* peek into a pocketbook, however, because this behavior falls into an entirely different category of snooping and might get you arrested.)

Peeking can be enlightening and fun, but it is always important to remember, in your excitement, to be careful not to get caught. No one will be happy to find you unzipping his gym bag, and you will not be able to explain why you are doing it. You cannot, for example, say, "Oh sorry, Just wanted to try to figure out whether or not you're a fag."

Ms. Behavior has used this technique herself twice. In one instance, a male coworker continued to be oblique far too long for Ms. Behavior's scanty patience. A glimpse into his bag revealed a jockstrap, a pair of shorts, a T-shirt, and . . . a bottle of Nair. Bingo! In another instance, which reveals Ms. Behavior's affinity for detective work, she caught a peek of some Chanel pour Homme cologne in a female coworker's gym bag. Score! Ms. Behavior could barely contain her glee at her newfound enlightenment. Each time she looked at her coworker from then on, she inhaled deeply, as if to say, "I smell you and I know who you are."

It is another Wednesday afternoon. After the trip to Macy's with her mother, Ms. Behavior has found that she truly cannot stop thinking about the stunning lesbian with the Pre-Raphaelite hair, so she returns to the store, as promised, on several consecutive Wednesdays. Finally, on the fifth Wednesday, she spots the goddess in the lingerie section, but pretends not to notice. Ms. Behavior anxiously fingers the first silky bra she can reach as the Beautiful One approaches from behind and taps her on the shoulder. "Didn't I see you at the Melissa Etheridge concert?" she asks breathily.

Ms. Behavior is nervous and clutches the bra to her chest. "No, I wasn't there," she says. "It must have been someone who looks like me. Lots of people look like me." She hurries toward the cash register.

"I can see that you are purchasing a bra in a 34B, which happens to be my size," the goddess says, keeping pace with Ms. Behavior. "I don't think it will fit you," she adds, after quickly assessing Ms. Behavior's ample breasts, "so perhaps you will let me borrow it."

"How did you know I was a lesbian?" Ms. Behavior blurts happily. The goddess never answers, but Ms. Behavior does not mind. She pays for the bra and gives it to her lovely new friend. They leave the store together.

Part Five

SEX

&

DATING

Chapter Twenty-Eight

✦ ✦ ✦

CONDOM ETIQUETTE
AND NEGOTIATING
SAFER SEX

*W*ho wants to eat the meat with the wrapping on it?
One of the advantages of being gay or lesbian used to be that you didn't have to bring extra apparatus to bed, unless it was an implement of pleasure, some kind of book or toy or video that might bring you to new heights of arousal and sensation. Gay men were the secret envy of straight ones, because not only was sex without commitment readily available, they also never had to bother with the horrors of latex.

On more than one occasion, Ms. Behavior's straight female friends have also bemoaned their fate at having to struggle with various birth control devices, to the point where some have even expressed the wish that they could be magically transformed into lesbians.

Ms. Behavior realizes that safer sex requires a sense of humor, because while it is the healthy and beautiful thing to do, it takes some getting used to. With AIDS as the great equalizer, enshrouding oneself in protective covering is part of the fun, fun, fun of sex for us all. Or at least we're supposed to aspire to that upbeat attitude.

Convincing your partner that safer sex is fun, fun, fun is where your sense of humor comes in. If serious conversation doesn't work, coercing a reluctant lover to use a condom can be accomplished through joking and teasing. Ms. Behavior's talented friend Harry has learned to put a condom on his partner with his lips and tongue. Harry learned this cool trick from a prostitute named Monique, and his lucky bedmates, who are impressed with Harry's oral dexterity, usually laugh. (Ms. Behavior wonders if you've ever noticed that laughing leads to more intense orgasms.)

Gay men may complain about safe sex ("I miss that hot, wet feeling," laments Tommy-Tuna), but whether they are constant in its practice or not, most at least believe it is necessary. Lesbians are a more recalcitrant bunch, because it is hard to convince them that they are at risk.

Gay men have the advantage of barriers that were actually designed for the purpose of boffing. Since condoms have been in existence for hundreds of years, they are refined in their function and have been tested for safety. Gay men also have a variety of choices that make sexual contact pleasurable: lubricated condoms for anal sex, unlubricated condoms for oral sex, and extra-large condoms for those with big members (or egos), for whom regular rubbers might be too much of a rub. (Ms. Behavior suggests that you try not to laugh and point to your partner's penis when he whips out a jumbo condom; this might shrivel his self-esteem.)

Lesbians, however, for the most part have been forced to resort to using things that are not actually intended to protect them during sexual contact but rather for covering a casserole or for use during oral surgery.

Ms. Behavior believes that dental dams are fine for dentists but are not very well designed for sapphic pleasure. First of all, they are thick. Place one of these over your vulva and try to feel your own finger, never mind your partner's delicate tongue.

Then there is the matter of the size. Designed to isolate a single tooth in dentistry and protect it from exposure to moisture and bacteria, dental dams are meant to cover a *small* area. When used for safer oral sex, they are supposed to keep you from coming in contact with your partner's vaginal fluid. Ms. Behavior would like to point out that she has noticed that the problem with these tiny dental dams is that some women are very wet. Perhaps she is going too far in mentioning specifics, but she has seen women drip down onto their thighs or up onto their abdomens. This is to say (totally scientifically, of course) that the expanse of wetness generated by a particular woman can greatly exceed the zone that the dental dam might cover. In order to protect enough area to keep you from the possibility of inadvertently slipping into a dampish place, Ms. Behavior suspects, a dental dam would have to be the size of a circus tent, or at least a pillowcase.

Dental dams are also difficult to keep in place. At least one of the partners has to hold the latex square with her hands, which can be inconvenient in terms of lovemaking. Still, Ms. Behavior suggests that you refrain from the impulse to use thumbtacks to keep the dental dam from sliding around.

Latex panties serve the same function as dental dams but tend to be a little thinner and easier to use, and you don't have to hold them in place. Like condoms, they come in various flavors and sizes. Since they do not afford you the comfort and breathability of regular cotton underwear, it's probably better not to wear them all day and then have your partner lick through them. Instead, you might want to don them just before making love.

Ms. Behavior has been to safer sex lectures where the educator demonstrated how lesbians can snip the ends off a condom and cut it open into a flat sheet to place over their partner's vulva. A resounding chorus of "Eeeewwww" and "Yuck" filled the room. This reaction apparently happened because some lesbians object to using condoms, even in a cut-up fashion; to such women, condoms represent men and a society of penises. To these wimmin, Ms. Behavior would politely say, "Get over it, missy." She would also remind you that if a condom is freshly packaged, no penis has ever had the pleasure of touching it. So try not to scream.

Ms. Behavior is sorry to report that she has developed a fetish for sheer plastic. Although it is not what the makers of Saran Wrap intended, lots of lesbians have been locking in freshness and, they hope, locking out HIV by using plastic wrap as a barrier during oral sex. (It can also be used for rimming; if you don't know what that is, ask your mother.) One of the primary drawbacks of the Saran Wrap method of safer sex, however, is that once you start doing it on a regular basis, you will find that you get sexually aroused every time you put away leftovers. The mere sound of tearing plastic will awaken your libido. Ms. Behavior's friend Lucy was at dinner party, watching the hostess put the food away at the end of the evening. Suddenly she seized a plate of carefully wrapped turkey and began to lick the shiny plastic wrap. With just this one slip, Lucy has ceased to be a popular dinner guest, and her social life has been ruined.

But Ms. Behavior believes that some things are just not worth worrying about. There seems to be some concern, for example, about whether nonmicrowavable wrap is better than microwavable wrap in terms of safer sex. This question seems to have evolved from the fact that microwavable wrap becomes porous at 300 degrees Fahrenheit. If you are a woman who reaches that temperature during lovemaking, please call Ms. Behavior. She would like to meet you.

Chapter Twenty-Nine

✦ ✦ ✦

HOW MS. BEHAVIOR LOST HER PESKY VIRGINITY, AND HOW YOU CAN LOSE YOURS

At age nineteen, Ms. Behavior was mortified by the fact that she was still a lesbian virgin. She had kissed a woman the year before, and felt geeky about its having been just a short pressing of lips beneath the bright lights in her friend's driveway. She knew that if she were really cool, she would have been ready for more, instead of quickly ejecting her friend from the car and driving off into the night.

During the following year, Ms. Behavior began to watch the lesbians around her carefully (luckily, there was no shortage of them to observe at Smith College), noticing how casually they touched each other, how sweetly they embraced. The parts she could envision but not see, however, were the most alluring; in Ms. Behavior's vivid imagination, all of the lesbians spent hot candelit nights with their limbs sensually entwined and their lips and tongues gently touching, while she slept alone on her hard, narrow cot.

Still, Ms. Behavior knew that her longing was not just about sex; her romantic sensibility prevented her from seeking only that. Ms. Behavior wanted to be in love. She imagined a lovely sepia-tinted scene in which she would hold a warm, soft body in her arms for the first time and cry, breathing in the sweet scent of hair and skin.

Late in the spring semester of that year, Ms. Behavior finally lost her lesbian virginity, to a woman she loved. She had spent the previous few months lying in bed with Julie, just talking and drinking beer. Since they were both naive and inexperienced, Ms. Behavior and Julie whispered things to each other like "I'm not really a lesbian — I just love you." And then they would kiss tentatively, stroke each other's hair, and get too nervous to allow things to evolve further. (Ms. Behavior was not sure she was being truthful about not being a lesbian, but Julie apparently was — she recently married a man).

Unfortunately, the night It happened was the beginning of Parents' Visiting Weekend at school. After going out to dinner with her parents on Friday night, Ms. Behavior came back and slipped into Julie's bed, where Julie was waiting, naked. This first night of passion was sweet and tender, and Ms. Behavior spent the rest of the weekend walking around in a fog, her mind flooded with erotic images. The problem was that the thrill of it all rendered her temporarily unable to speak, and while her parents kept trying to get her to show them around the campus and talk about her classes and grades, all she could do was think of Julie's naked body and say "Mmmmmm." Finally, the horrendous tension ended with Ms. Behavior's parents accusing her of being on drugs and leaving early, in a huff.

The old axiom that timing is everything is true. If you happen to be a gay or lesbian virgin, Ms. Behavior advises you, given her own experience, *not* to combine your first weekend of love and romance with a visit from your parents. It is worse than repulsive.

In any case, if you are over the age of eighteen, you have probably already realized that your virginity is a burden. If you are unlucky enough to be a gay or lesbian virgin, Ms. Behavior's tender heart goes out to you, because virginity breeds virginity, which means it's unlikely you'll be getting any anytime soon. (Ms. Behavior is obviously not referring to virginity in the traditional heterosexual sense, but rather in the sense of whether or not you have had a same-sex encounter.)

To put this another way, the problem with being a virgin is that normal people are usually wary of sleeping with one. This attitude presents a dilemma, similar to the one you might come up against in looking for a job when you have no experience: No one wants to hire you, so how are you supposed to get trained? Sex and economics are very closely linked in many ways; with sex, as with money, the more you have, the more you get.

People don't mean to reject you for your virginity. They just fear that (a) if they give you your first beautiful sexual experience, you might fall hopelessly in love with them and become a cling-on, suction-cup pest, or (b) they might fall hopelessly in love with you, only to find that your previous sexual deprivation combined with a thirst for education makes you want to spend the next several years cultivating as many sexual experiences as possible while they wait miserably for you to return.

The only people who are exceptions to this rule of virgin-avoidance are those you would not want near you: the truly twisted individuals who want the unsullied and would consider you a notch on their well-worn bedposts, or the indisputably HIV-paranoid, who will doubt your purity anyway and make you cover your entire body, including your arms and legs, with latex and spray you with disinfectant before touching you. Believe Ms. Behavior when she tells you that you do not want your first sexual experience to take place at the hands of either of these types.

So how do you find a nice, normal person who will relieve you of your virginity? Well, so far as Ms. Behavior can tell, you have only two choices. You can either try to find a sweet and understanding person, get to know him really well, wait until you are quite sure that he is totally taken with you, and then let him know that you have saved yourself for someone as special as he is, or you can lie and pretend to be experienced.

If you are so lucky as to find someone who is kind enough not to mind your virginity, this is the best route, since you can allow him to treat you as the novice that you are. You will not have to endure the hardship of trying to pretend to know what you are doing, on top of the nervousness that naturally exists anyway your first time.

If you rip the condom in half when you open the wrapper with your teeth, or if you spit the first time you taste a dental dam, your kind partner might not laugh. Under the best of circumstances, your seducteur might be gentle and generous and willing to teach you some fabulous tricks. In such an ideal scenario, your partner will feel powerful but tender, and you will feel cared for.

If, however, you choose the lying route and pretend to be experienced, you may end up feeling embarrassed. Although you are no doubt naturally endowed with wonderful instincts for lovemaking, you might be somewhat clumsy and fumbling the first time or two, which could cause your unsuspecting partner (whom you have just turned over as if on a rotisserie or poked in the eye with your elbow) to assume you are simply a bad lover. The repercussions of this are worse than you might think; the gay and lesbian grapevine is such that you might never be able to date again in this country without changing your name and appearance. (Ms. Behavior envisions a business opportunity in starting the Bad Lover Relocation Program.) Even worse, you would also lose the opportunity to allow your partner to try to make it a beautiful experience for you.

Whatever you do, do not acknowledge your inexperience but then try to downplay it by saying that you have watched a lot of X-rated movies or read a lot of sexually explicit books. People will just laugh at you (even before you take off your clothes).

Ms. Behavior sometimes receives letters from young lesbians who ask her to be their first lover. She usually responds by saying she would rather have something sharp shoved under her fingernails. Ms. Behavior is not saying it's impossible; she is just saying that in order to have Ms. Behavior as your first lover, you would have to do something drastic, like make her fall in love with you.

If you succeeded, however, and Ms. Behavior were your first lover, she would rub your body with oil and look into your eyes lovingly. She would stroke your hair while k.d. lang played in the background and calm your anxiety by whispering sweet things into your ear. She would teach you all of her sexual secrets and would slowly and sweetly initiate you into the universal club of lesbians. And although she would be too embarrassed to tell her friends about it and would swear you to eternal secrecy, it would be a tender and beautiful experience and one Ms. Behavior surely would cherish.

Chapter Thirty

✦ ✦ ✦

FINDING TRUE LOVE
THROUGH THE
PERSONALS

*I*f she could, Ms. Behavior would write personal ads for a living. She would feel completely fulfilled in her career as a personal-ad writer, because she believes in generating happiness. It would also satisfy her secret desire to have a unique job, and since no one has ever hired her to be in charge of issuing fragrance violations to people wearing copycat cologne, which is her optimal employment fantasy, she would gladly settle for this. Anyway, if you hired Ms. Behavior to write your ad, she would always present you as a superb catch and would do her best to bring passionate love and romantic enchantment to your lonely little life, you Hot, Passionate, Hard-Bodied GM, Seeking Same. (But Ms. Behavior is sorry to report that she cannot write ads promoting you as a Human Sucking Machine. It would make her squeamish.)

You will most likely be stuck with the task of writing your own ad, however, so Ms. Behavior will try to convey the most important elements of ad creation. Be forewarned that this can be an emotionally trying job, requiring you to push beyond fear and self-conscious-ness. Writing the ad can feel a lot like walking naked through the center of town, near your old elementary school.

Once you start writing, a dark cloud will settle around your head. You will think of all the reasons that your previous relationships have not worked and blame yourself for everything. For example, you will think, "Well, I am hard working. I can include that," and then you will remember that your last lover hated the fact that you spent so much time at the office, called your secretary to complain, and even sent hate mail addressed to your office, since you were never home to talk about it.

So you cross out "hardworking" and decide to include "creative" in your ad, but then you think about how another ex-lover looked at you blankly when you shared your poetry, and for your birthday, after you expressed a desire to cultivate your artistic talent, bought you a paint-by-numbers set.

Describing yourself in a personal ad can be tricky, because it is all about selling yourself. It is much easier, in fact, to write an ad selling your car, because you can say that it is hot, has low mileage, and is reliable and fast. If you said the same of yourself, you might feel afraid of being challenged.

Ms. Behavior has to tell you that it is very hard to try to sell something you don't love. (Now Ms. Behavior is channeling Louise Hay.) The point is not necessarily to cultivate higher self-esteem prior to writing your ad, although that would be nice. Instead of spending all that time, energy, and therapy trying to feel better about yourself (which could take years), why not take a shortcut and let a friend write your personal ad for you? Your friend will not be as self-con-scious as you are, and will probably be more familiar with your attributes anyway. He or she will have no trouble describing you as sexy, intelligent, and amazingly witty, which you might be too shy or self-deprecating to do (even if it happens to be true).

Letting a friend write an ad for you involves trust. But you should always have the final say about what will run in the paper, since even your closest friends can be a little weird sometimes. When Ms. Behavior's friends wrote a personal ad for her, they made her sound like a horse: "Tall, attractive, green-eyed lesbian, with good teeth and bone structure . . ." Ms. Behavior was appalled. She got three responses from dentists and two from veterinarians.

When she asked her friends to rewrite the ad, focusing more on emotional characteristics than physical ones, they described her as an "attractive, bossy, independent, witty, green-eyed lesbian writer, who likes to get her own way." Well, that description primarily attracted responses from women who wrote expressing their desire to be tied to the bedpost or dominated in some other, even less subtle way.

Do not under any circumstances consult family members about what to say about you in a personal ad. They will make you sound like some kind of dweeb with no sex appeal, and will exaggerate your weaknesses. Your ad would read something like this: "Smart, handsome boy who learned to read at age three, messy at mealtimes, with a good heart and kindness toward kittens, seeks nice girl (oops, we mean boy) for sharing ice cream, movies, and visiting relatives."

Sometimes it's best to let someone who doesn't know you *too* well write the ad. That way, her reactions to your quirky ways will not poke through in some kind of subtle but revealing way. It is best to ask someone who knows enough about you to make you sound appealing but is distant enough so that she is still somewhat infatuated and admiring. If you have a friend like that, though, the obvious question is, why aren't you two dating?

No matter who writes your ad for you, you'll want to maintain a careful balance between openness and mystery. Tell as much as you need to tell to paint an alluring picture, but don't go over the top and reveal too much. It is best to keep your neuroses to yourself until the other person is ensnared by your web (oops, Ms. Behavior means charm). Plus, you want to find out who this person is before you expose too much of yourself.

Ms. Behavior's friend Lucy got a very enticing response to her ad, from a woman who called herself Madame X. Over a period of months, Lucy and Madame X talked frequently on the phone and through letters, becoming quite close. They planned several meetings, which the raspy-voiced Madame X kept postponing because she was recovering from throat surgery and wanted to wait until she healed. When Lucy was finally due to visit, her correspondent said that she had "something to tell her." It turned out, of course, that Madame X was a man, whose deep voice was due to testosterone.

Poor Oogie was also duped by a personal-ad lie. The man who responded to his ad claimed to be an Olympic athlete visiting from Sweden. It was only after four telephone conversations that Oogie realized that the familiar accent belonged to his geeky eighth-grade science teacher, whose only athletic endeavors involved number-two pencils and calculators.

Sometimes answering a personal ad is easier and less expensive than placing one. Remember that humor is key, because you need to make your response stand out. Ms. Behavior's friend Penelope answered an ad from a woman who described herself as "tiny" by saying she had always wanted a pocket girlfriend. The woman called to inquire if Penelope kept diamonds in her pocket. Penelope responded by asking if the woman was small enough to carry in her mouth to work, and if she could spit her out on the desk when she got there. Tiny fell silent for a few moments, and Penelope got nervous thinking she had offended her, but Tiny resumed the conversation by singing the Lollipop Guild song. Now Penelope and the lovely Tiny have been together three blissful lesbian years. The unexpected factor in all this is that Tiny weighs in at three hundred. (She doesn't spit anything out.)

Do not be afraid to place or answer personal ads out of concern that it makes you seem desperate. Personal ads are a way of specifying the characteristics you want in a lover, and who knows? You might just be lucky enough to find them. Besides, it seems less desperate than standing around a bar with a hungry, leering look on your face (which, despite your protests, you *do* develop by the end of the evening).

What's the worst thing that can happen, besides the very occasional brutal murder? A truly miserable personal-ad date makes a riveting story to tell at a party. People are always attracted to the horror element of such things, so when you tell your tale, they will be fascinated, as if they have come upon a train wreck. Ms. Behavior only wishes she didn't know this firsthand.

Chapter Thirty-One

✦ ✦ ✦

WHAT TO DO WHEN A
STRAIGHT PERSON
SETS HIS OR HER
SIGHTS ON YOU

Dear Ms. Behavior:

I have been corresponding with a woman whom I met through a personal ad several months ago. Nancy lives on the West Coast, and although we have never met in person, we have been writing to each other every day and speak frequently on the phone. I am thrilled to be flying to San Francisco at the end of the month to meet her.

The problem, Ms. Behavior, is that Nancy is straight. She is married to a Marine and lives right near the base. She has three kids. Still, she says that she has fallen in love with me, and has been expressing some pretty wild sexual desires, too. I constantly fantasize about what it might be like to be her first lover. We have had phone sex numerous times, which has been wonderful. Still, I find myself feeling very nervous about this.

Ms. Behavior, I have a list of questions that I need your advice about.

1. What do straight women like in bed? 2. Should I make love to her all night, or should I let her sleep a little too? 3. What should I wear during the weekend? (I only have dykey clothing and work clothing, and I am afraid that either might be scary.) 4. Is it necessary for me to shave my armpits? (It would feel like a major compromise, but if you think it is important, I will do it. I shaved them for my brother's wedding, and I felt bad about it afterwards.)

Thanks for your help with this, Ms. Behavior.

— Can't Help Myself

Dear Can't Help Myself:

Ms. Behavior's assessment is that you are either (a) going through a period of karmic hell or (b) a glutton for punishment. Getting emotionally involved with a straight person guarantees disaster. If you choose not to heed Ms. Behavior's large shaking finger of warning, be prepared to spend a fortune on Kleenex, Pepto-Bismol, and night-time sleep aids.

Your first question is very easy to answer. What do straight women like in bed? Men!!! As flexible, as butch, and as eager to please as you might be, and regardless of your accessories, you will not be able to achieve the level of manhood that your straight woman desires. You will just end up on the Sally Jesse Raphael show with a caption under your face that says "Not Man Enough for a Straight Woman."

In your next greedy inquiry, you ask if you should make love to her all night or let her sleep a little. Do you aspire to replace the Energizer bunny? If you insist on making love with a straight woman, Ms. Behavior would suggest that you try not to exceed a reasonable two-hour time limit. That will allow you to leave a few tricks in your bag so that she might remain curious enough to give you another tumble, which you will probably masochistically desire. A two-hour limit may also provide you with enough sleep to survive the emotional hell she is likely to put you through the next day.

What you wear is not really relevant, except to you. When the straight woman looks at you, it is as if she is looking at a creature from Pluto. All she can see are your real or imagined dykey features, plus the sign around your neck that reads GIANT LESBO. You could wear a spacesuit and it wouldn't matter. In fact, you may as well, because if you wear your favorite outfit, you will always associate it with the straight woman, and after she dumps you, you will find it too painful ever to wear it again. (Ms. Behavior unfortunately knows this from her own experience. She still gags at the smell of Paco Rabanne because she wore it during her breakup with her second lover, who also happened to be a straight woman.)

Some of your lesbian lovers may have enjoyed lightly running their fingers through your plush armpit hair. Well, straight women are just not like that. Leaving it or shaving it is up to you, but Ms. Behavior can pretty much guarantee that the first moment you lift your arm, revealing a mass of tangled hair, your straight woman will leap out of bed in a big hurry, clutching her clothing against her body. Straight women are downright squeamish about things like body hair.

Ms. Behavior wonders what your straight woman will do with her Marine during your weekend of lascivious love. Does he get to stand at attention and watch?

Ms. Behavior always takes it as a a sign of trouble when a straight person has an ache that can be quelled by nothing other than eating the forbidden fruit from your personal vine. Bear in mind that you are naked. Bear in mind that this person is a snake. Try to remember that the world is filled with millions of authentic lesbians, many of whom are lonely and would feel happy to be blessed with your love and company.

If the straight person says, "I know I am not really gay, but I am just in love with you," clamp your hands over your ears and sing. It is your only hope for salvation.

Ms. Behavior understands that the appeal of being someone's first lies in the warm feeling that rises in your chest when a chaste person looks to you for guidance and help. The innocent person reaching out toward the wise teacher — it makes you feel like Jesus. It makes you feel chosen. Still, Ms. Behavior suggests that you instead derive your feelings of fulfillment from beautifying your neighborhood or rescuing stray animals.

The one crucial question you neglected to ask was whether or not you should go ahead with the visit. Ms. Behavior suspects that this is because you have decided to go, no matter what. You're a big girl. Go to San Francisco. Just do not come crying to Ms. Behavior, expecting to rest your head on her ample bosom after the straight babe dumps you and breaks your heart into a hundred tiny pieces.

Chapter Thirty-Two

✦ ✦ ✦

FALLING IN LOVE

WITH THE WRONG TYPE

When Ms. Behavior was a teenager and had just begun to date boys (before her lesbianism really took hold), her family offered her one piece of minimalist wisdom about romance: "It's just as easy to fall in love with someone rich as someone poor." (Despite the repeated reinforcement of this suggestion, Ms. Behavior did not choose boys based on the size of their allowances.) That one tidbit, the only familial guidance Ms. Behavior ever received regarding relationships, apparently had little long-term influence; most of the women Ms. Behavior has loved have earned barely enough money to keep themselves in Gap T-shirts and rice cakes.

Although Ms. Behavior's more romantic side believes that love is like a runaway train and there is no sense in trying to choose whom you love, her practical side wants to believe that the rational mind can exert some influence. Assuming it is possible to control the experience, Ms. Behavior advises you to fall in love with a decorator or a record promoter, for example, rather than a personal trainer or a psychotherapist. If you think that the opportunistic Ms. Behavior is merely implying that a decorator might provide you with lovely surroundings and a record promoter with lots of cultural opportunities, you are only partially right. The more important part of this advice is rooted in valuing not money or social standing but such intangible rewards as clear boundaries, aesthetic satisfaction, and, most important, maintaining your own sanity.

Falling in love with the wrong type, however, will be quite tempting. One day you will be lying on your back on a bench in the gym and your personal trainer will be standing over you murmuring encouraging words like "That's right. It's all you, baby. Now *push*." As you feel your pecs tense and your muscles tighten, your trainer's voice will sound beautiful and soothing. It will feel like a soft and firm hand across your skin, a gentle breeze across your sweaty face. Your eyes rest on his beautifully sculpted body, which is covered with a fine mist of sweat, and your blood suddenly turns hot. You nearly drop the barbell on your face.

Ms. Behavior would like to remind you that you are only having a feeling, which, if ignored, will pass. Do not act on the desire to ask your trainer to come home with you and do not beg him to please throw his sweaty workout clothing on your bed for the rest of his days. While the thought of having him put you through an entirely different kind of exercise routine may seem erotic at first, it will grow tiresome after the first three or four episodes of him barking pushup commands in bed: "One and two and three and four . . ." Within a week or two, you will begin to associate sexuality with strained muscles and torn ligaments. Once that happens, you will either leave, so that your body can recover, or grow addicted to this painful association, which will force you to live the remainder of your life as an s/m queen, looking for the ultimate pain-pleasure connection. (Ms. Behavior does not mean to imply that s/m is bad or wrong, only that if it's not what you're already into, it will require buying a whole new expensive leather and metal wardrobe and changing your name to Spike, Daddy, or the Gimp.)

Ms. Behavior offers an equally stern warning about dating anyone whom you have employed in a professional capacity, ranging from your accountant to your gynecologist to your therapist.

Your accountant knows way too much about your finances (or lack of them) to be an appropriate lover. Besides, accountants are generally boring, obsessive people to live with. They are consumed with picky details and will keep track of things like who took out the garbage last, how many times you have made love in a given month, and how many cents you would save each week by buying a cheap cereal that you don't like nearly as much as the expensive one you regularly eat. Your cabinets will be overflowing with dishwasher liquid and mouthwash, since they force you to buy everything in bulk.

And although you may be tempted by your sweet, soft-spoken gynecologist as she examines your cervix, do not even think about asking her on a date. First of all, Ms. Behavior advises against dating anybody who has seen any part of your body that you can't see yourself without special equipment. The power imbalance is too great. Your gynecologist knows your body too intimately and too objectively for you to feel sexy around her. Every time she touched your breasts in bed, you would know that she was surreptitiously examining you. And just as you were about to give yourself over totally to the experience of making love, you would remember that her hands are inside fifty women's gowns each day!

Ms. Behavior should not have to issue a warning about dating your therapist, but apparently she does, since there seems to be a growing club of people who have spent the wrong kind of time on the psychotherapy couch. Do not count on your therapist to be the one who is able to uphold professional boundaries; some do not know how. If your therapist offers to take you out for ice cream after a difficult session, get another therapist. And if you are at a concert and you hear a familiar voice that sounds like your therapist's rising above all the others, singing "Kumbaya," locate the nearest exit and run.

This may sound harsh, but Ms. Behavior actually suggests not only that you not date your own therapist but that you stay away from *any* psychotherapist, particularly one who is psychoanalytic in approach. Once, when Ms. Behavior dated Cynthia, a doctoral student in psychology, she told Cynthia that she felt Cynthia's dog needed more walks and attention. Cynthia responded by saying that she felt that perhaps Ms. Behavior was projecting her own needs onto the dog and that Ms. Behavior probably needed more love and attention. That night she tried to ask Ms. Behavior questions about her childhood, probing for reasons that Ms. Behavior might feel unloved. Ms. Behavior promptly got down on the floor and barked.

Although it is hard for Ms. Behavior to acknowledge, honesty and integrity force her to warn you about dating etiquette and advice columnists. Advice columnists are very picky people who notice everything you do, and they have to be right all the time. Plus, you are always in danger of being the embarrassing topic of next week's column. If you and your lover have a fight about your mother, it will end up in her column. If you have a tiff about how often you're having sex, you might see it in print. Anything you do or say is examined through the filter of whether it is good material or not, and sometimes your advice-columnist lover will allow weird things to happen, or even create odd and uncomfortable situations, just to be able to use them.

So who's left? People who work as artists tend to be interesting lovers, as long as they can support themselves and are not too anguished about life. But stay away from the artists or writers who are totally self-obsessed or the ones who romanticize pain and death. (A huge collection of books by people like Sylvia Plath and Anne Sexton tends to be a bad sign, as is artwork by such depressives as van Gogh.)

Teachers tend to be kind and patient people, as do nurses, though both groups may be injudicious in their use of the pronoun "we." Be careful of veterinarians, dog groomers, or anyone too closely involved with animals; they tend to be petcentric and talk in high-pitched voices, as if speaking for their four-legged friends. Ms. Behavior used to leave her dog with a cute lesbian dog groomer. She soon noticed that she could never date a woman like this, however, because every time she picked up her dog, she would find the dog and the groomer sharing a Slurpy.

So much of your perception of someone is, of course, about projection. Your own hopes and expectations cannot help but color your vision. But Ms. Behavior must remind you that when you first meet someone, there is always a moment of clarity, a moment when you see that person unencumbered by all of your own projections. It is like the moment after a nose job, when the surgeon hands the patient a mirror and he or she can see the new nose, before all the swelling that creates incredible distortion. Ms. Behavior advises you to use that moment of clarity wisely. Because once all that swelling happens between you and a prospective lover, your vision is impaired, and you won't make a single good decision until months or years later, when everything shrinks down to normal size.

Chapter Thirty-Three

✦　✦　✦

FATAL ATTRACTION:
ARE YOU DATING A
BUNNY BOILER?

B e careful what you pray for; you might get it.

Ms. Behavior is still sorry for having lamented one day that there was no woman on the planet who was obsessed with her, no person whose day was filled with longing for her. Ms. Behavior was bored with her life, and she made a stupid statement. "All I want," Ms. Behavior recalls saying to her friend Penelope over dinner, "is a *Fatal Attraction* kind of love. I want a woman who will drive by my house fifty times a day, just to see if I am home. I want her to call my answering machine just to hear my voice, to be tortured by desirous thoughts of me, to think and talk of nothing but me." In retrospect, Ms. Behavior cannot remember whether she was joking.

A few weeks later, Ms. Behavior met Jeanette. Ms. Behavior never should have kissed Jeanette, especially once they had spent an evening together and Ms. Behavior knew that she was not interested in future dates. But you know how it is, between relationships, when that thick ennui sets in and you think you might never meet anyone you *really* want to kiss again, so you find yourself pinned beneath a warm, relatively attractive body in your car, your head jammed between the steering wheel and the seat.

The fact that Ms. Behavior allowed Jeanette's tongue into her mouth was probably poor judgment. That she allowed Jeanette's palms to press against her breasts was a terrible mistake. Still, after a little controlled necking in Ms. Behavior's big matronmobile, she never really expected to see Jeanette again.

Once someone has had her mouth pressed to yours for twenty or thirty minutes, it is difficult to convince her the next day that you are not really interested in pursuing a relationship. She still remembers the feeling of your fingers in her hair, your warm breath on her cheek, and she thinks you are lying, nervous, or — Ms. Behavior's favorite — fearful of intimacy. She believes that if only you lay eyes on her again, you will remember just how much you like her. So your stubborn pursuer sets out to achieve the single-minded goal of one more date.

Jeanette's phone calls were incessant. No matter how busy or uninterested Ms. Behavior said she was, Jeanette persisted. All Ms. Behavior could think to do was to decline politely and thank the Goddess that she hadn't slept with this wackadoo. Not that it would have made much difference, apparently.

Just as it seemed that Jeanette might finally be giving up, Ms. Behavior went one night to her mother's house for dinner. She had just noticed that there was an extra setting at the kitchen table when Jeanette emerged from the hallway, wearing a white lace dress and lots of makeup, with her hair piled high in some sort of fancy up-do. Ms. Behavior immediately started choking on her Evian.

"I'll bet you're surprised to see me," Jeanette said, approaching the table and kissing Ms. Behavior's stunned face. "Your mom, Bubbles, is so sweet. She insisted that I come to dinner and surprise you."

Ms. Behavior later found out that Jeanette had called Bubbles earlier that week in an attempt to track her down. Jeanette had explained to Bubbles that she and Ms. Behavior just could not seem to connect, and how sad they both were that they kept missing each other. By the end of the conversation, Jeanette had also told Bubbles how lucky Ms. Behavior was to have such a lovely mother, since her own mother had died in a car wreck when she was a child.

Bubbles, of course, was moved to tears by Jeanette's tragic (if fictitious) tale and extended an invitation to Jeanette to be the surprise dinner guest that night. She was also ready to adopt her. Ms. Behavior had no choice but to feign an attack of stomach virus and go home before the entrée was served, leaving Jeanette and Bubbles to entertain each other.

Ms. Behavior hopes you understand why it is bad to wish for someone to be obsessed with you, and thinks that if you ever find a genie in a bottle, you should stick with the ordinary requests, like money, fame, and multiple orgasms. If someone does become obsessed with you, you should recognize that this unwanted attention will be not easy to discourage; a person who is obsessed will be relentless and creative and will do anything to win your affection. Your only choice is to try to be equally creative in your escape and not to worry too much about hurting the bunny boiler's feelings.

It will not work, for example, to try to turn away the fatal attractionist by saying that you value your friendship so much that you don't want to risk losing it. Any living, breathing person knows that that line is a lie, and such condescension will only serve to infuriate. In some ways, it is better to tell the truth: "I cannot envision being with you. You are not really my type." Or "I just do not feel any chemistry with you. I am sure you are a nice person, but you're not someone with whom I want to eat my next several thousand dinners."

Your obsessive suitor may try to prove you wrong, which will be tedious. He or she may ask you endless questions about what you really want in a lover and try to become that kind of person. You must make it clear that there are no external things that will make a difference, so that your obsessor does not have to go through the added indignation of wearing shoe lifts, buying Armani suits, changing his or her cologne, or adopting a southern drawl. If you think this person has zero chance of winning your affection as a lover, it is best to say so from the start.

Ms. Behavior's friend Alex was pursued endlessly in college by a man named Fred. Fred hung signs around the campus proclaiming his love and stood beneath Alex's window singing love songs in Italian. During a big snowstorm, when Alex walked by his dorm, Fred jumped out of his third-floor window into a snowdrift in an attempt to impress. The fact that this feat broke his leg only slowed Fred down briefly; by the next day he had found an artist to paint Alex's picture on his cast. Alex got no relief until he graduated and moved far away, with no forwarding address.

Obviously, if you are being pursued by a real stalker, you need to involve those folks who wear blue uniforms and carry guns. But at a lesser level, one that is just chronically annoying, Ms. Behavior has some suggestions:

1. Be direct in rejecting his advances. Tell him that you are not interested and never will be.

2. If he continues to be relentless, call him by the wrong name when you see him, as if you cannot remember who he is.

3. If forced to engage in conversation, choose a close and relaxed moment for the following disclosure: Since traveling to various countries last summer, you have discovered that Americans are far too hung up about things like hygiene, and you now think showering once a week is more than sufficient. Reveal your knowledge that body odor was designed for one animal to attract another, and elaborate on how sexy you think pungent bodily scents are. If the person gets a lustful look on his face, your plan is backfiring. Quickly try another tack.

4. Develop some unappealing habits. You can chew loudly, pick things off your face at the dinner table, scratch your head a lot, pick your ears. (Nose picking is too overt and disgusting, so don't do it.)

5. For those truly recalcitrant cases, Ms. Behavior whips out a well-kept secret recipe for extinguishing the flames of unwanted passion. If you really can't get rid of the bunny boiler by any other means, you have to act crazier than he is. Call him at all hours of the night. Bother him at work. Send crazy mail and poems proclaiming your love. Try to get him to make an everlasting commitment to you. Tell him that you want to be the earth revolving around his sun. He will probably run like hell.

Chapter Thirty-Four

✦　✦　✦

SHOULD YOU EVER DO IT ON THE FIRST DATE?

*M*s. Behavior wonders if you have ever thought about sex in relation to Oreo cookies. Think about how some people nibble around the edges of the cookie and some take a big bite. Some people dunk the Oreo in milk to make it wet and soggy before eating it, letting it get soft and smooth against their tongue. And then there are those well-disciplined folks who gently take the cookie apart and slowly scrape the cream out with their teeth, savoring the part they like best.

Ms. Behavior suspects that the cookie eater who takes a big initial bite, then chews and swallows the cookie quickly, without prolonging the process in any way, has similar sexual habits. This would be the person who plunges right in on the first date and goes home feeling gratified and sated. (Or perhaps just bloated and nauseous.)

There you are on your first date with someone you find very appealing. You have talked and laughed over dinner; he has brushed his warm and manly hand against yours during the movie and even given you a light peck on the cheek during the walk back to your apartment. He's cute and charming. You know if you invite him in for coffee or a nightcap, you will end up taking off all your clothing and creating shadow puppets on the wall of your bedroom. As you approach your door, you have thirty seconds to decide whether or not to go for it.

This is a moment of mental anguish. You worry that if you invite him in, the date will evolve into a one-night stand and your chances of a relationship will turn to dust. Once you have both removed your clothing and gotten on with sex act #145, you could lose that interesting thread of conversation about fragrances, opera, and Asian cooking, never to regain it. Then, instead of leaving with the lovely lilt of your voice in his head, your hunky date will depart during the night, remembering only the somewhat impersonal sound of sighing and grunting, and you might never see him again.

There is something about getting naked with someone you don't really know that makes the evening seem to come full circle, as if you have completed something together and don't need anything more. This is not a moral issue, but one about missing out on the benefits of suspense and longing.

Conversely, you worry that if you do not invite your date in, he may take it as a signal that you are not interested or, if he is very insecure, that you can't stand his guts. In the meantime, before you have a chance to call to ask for another date, he might meet someone more forthcoming and fall in love. (Perhaps that will even happen on his way home, since he will be sad about not having been invited into your place.) Plus, maybe he'll think you're an old-fashioned prude, or just plain Not Fun.

Here is where some men might be helped by learning lesbian negotiating tactics, which allow you to express your true and earnest desire for your date while letting him know that he must keep his pants on. You say something like "I need to tell you that you make my heart beat fast and my knees buckle, and I would love to cover your body in berries and cream and feast on it. However, I would like to get to know the sweet and secret passageways in your mind first, and to sustain the longing and the pleasure of my intense desire for you, so that when our naked bodies finally do collide in unified pleasure, it will be the sensual highlight of my entire life, and will split the universe into tiny fiery fragments, ignited and exploded by our passion."

If your ordinary style of conversation is simpler and more direct, you might just say, "I like you very much but cannot consider doing the nasty with you tonight, because doing it on our first date would fuck up my head." Either approach will work if you can convey your sincere interest, and also your regret at being unable to follow through on your true desire.

With most people, sex is not necessary right away, so long as they know just how desperately you want them. Most people are ultimately more interested in your desire for them than they are in sex; actual lovemaking is much less important than knowledge of your urgent longing.

Lesbians have much less to worry about on a first date than gay men do, because they are not actually ever expected to make love until at least date number two. Lesbians are, however, expected to see whether they are cuddling compatible on the first date. If cuddling compatibility cannot be achieved, the second date never happens.

Cuddling compatibility is tested by sitting close on a loveseat and noticing whether your bodies fit nicely together when you hug and whether or not you are enraptured by the scent of your date's hair and the softness of her face. You imagine waking up next to her, with her legs wrapped around your hips, her breasts pressed into your back, her breath on your neck. If envisioning this does not make you feel wiggly inside, you don't need to worry about a next date.

You should beware if you are a lesbian on a first date and you happen to act on some sort of aberrant sexual impulse that your date happens to share: You may be making a long-term commitment. When lesbians have sex, it is as if they have symbolically exchanged rings. (Ms. Behavior wonders if this is a finger-related phenomenon.) You should remember that the first time you touch any lesbian in a

175

sexual manner, it is as if you are proclaiming your everlasting devotion. If that is not your intention, then keep your hands to yourself, because she will not understand — unless you happen to find one of those extremely rare lesbians who like to have sex for *fun*. If so, Ms. Behavior offers you her congratulations, her blessing, and her envy.

Unlike your friends, your parents, and even Ann Landers, Ms. Behavior does not think you will burn in the fiery pits of hell if you end up bumping uglies on the first date. As Ms. Behavior's Oreo analogy illustrates, while you might try to overcome your impulses, your inclination about sexual matters is aleady determined. So Ms. Behavior gently suggests that you do not torture yourself if you feel unable to follow through on your ideal image of yourself. In other words, if you happen to be a slut, Ms. Behavior suggests that you try to cultivate some self-acceptance and love yourself for your sluttiness.

And in case you were wondering about Ms. Behavior, she is the type of Oreo eater who likes to take very tiny bites for a while, teasing herself a bit until she is really hungry, and then she rips the cookie open with her teeth and pulls the sweet cream into her mouth.

Chapter Thirty-Five

✦ ✦ ✦

MS. BEHAVIOR LEARNS ABOUT CUT VS. UNCUT WIENERS OVER DINNER

*M*s. Behavior is out for dinner with some friends, discussing her book, which is nearly finished. Her friend Kenny suggests that Ms. Behavior has missed a topic that is crucial to gay male life: a chapter about circumcised versus uncircumcised penises. The following is the verbatim conversation.

Ms. BEHAVIOR: What's the big deal about this cut versus uncut thing, anyway? It's just a piece of skin, isn't it?

KENNY: It's not a piece of skin. It's a style.

PENELOPE: It's not something you can change, like your hair, so how can it be considered a style?

STEVE: It's just that uncut dicks are very in right now.

KENNY: Because ethnic-looking men are in. It's that exotic thing.

TOM: It might be a style of sorts. Men who are not happy with their circumcision can change back to natural if they stretch the skin or use weights.

STEVE: It takes years.

MS. BEHAVIOR: What's the point? Why bother?

STEVE: Because uncut dicks are sexy.

TOM: An uncut penis is just a dick with a turtleneck.

MS. BEHAVIOR: Why are they sexier, Steve?

STEVE: Because they are natural and manly. And if you're having sex with someone who's uncut, you know the person has heightened sensitivity, which is a turn-on.

MS. BEHAVIOR: Might you be uncut, Steve?

STEVE: Uh-huh.

PENELOPE: What about that cheesy stuff?

MS. BEHAVIOR: Eeewww.

KENNY: No one we hang out with would have that.

TOM: That's what you think.

STEVE: You just have to keep it clean, that's all.

PENELOPE: Eeeewwwww. Cheesy.

KENNY: How do you know it's more sensitive if you're uncut?

STEVE: I can tell.

TOM: How? By comparing it to your other, circumcised dick?

STEVE: No, by comparing it to your dick.

KENNY: I think at least uncut men have the advantage of a little lubrication inside the foreskin.

STEVE: Yeah, that's what makes even masturbating better with a foreskin. It feels like you're having sex.

MS. BEHAVIOR: Correct me if I'm wrong, but doesn't masturbation feel like sex to everyone?

STEVE: No.

KENNY: Yes.

PENELOPE: No.

TOM: Absolutely.

MS. BEHAVIOR: Okay, maybe it's like sex with someone you've been involved with for ten years, who doesn't really turn you on anymore.

STEVE: I still turn myself on.

KENNY: That's because you're in love with your own uncut penis, you pervert.

PENELOPE: Way back when I did boys, I think uncut penises were considered undesirable.

TOM: Well, it's different. You were never a gay man.

KENNY: Or were you?

MS. BEHAVIOR: Can we get back to the issue at hand?

KENNY: I think it's a matter of personal taste, so to speak. I have a friend who has three requirements in a boyfriend. He has to have no facial hair, be employed, and be cut.

TOM: He sounds like a very deep person.

Ms. BEHAVIOR: Well, maybe it's just a preference, the way eye color is.

PENELOPE: I would date a woman with eyes of any color.

TOM: Oh look. The waiter is here with our food.

WAITER: Here are your salads. Does anyone want any cheese on top?

TOM: No thanks.

STEVE: No.

KENNY: No.

Ms. BEHAVIOR: No thanks.

PENELOPE: No, and please cancel my Wiener schnitzel.

Chapter Thirty-Six

✦   ✦   ✦

FOR WOMEN ONLY: PENETRATION OR PENETRATION-FREE?

Way back in the seventies, when consciousness raising peaked and political correctness hit its stride, lots of lesbos eschewed the practice of allowing anything "in," so to speak. Clitoral sex was in and vaginal sex was out. In many feminist lesbian circles, being penetration-free was next to godliness. Penetration was considered an evil infiltration because it represented what straight people did in bed.

The aesthetics of the time were rigid, too. Lesbians tried to discard their predecessors' butch and femme uniforms and instead adopt one style as nearly universal. The majority of dykes started to dress in flannel shirts, jeans or carpenter pants, and Timberland boots. Alix Dobkin's song "Any Woman Can Be a Lesbian" played in bars and community centers. (The most memorable words to the song were "There's no penis between us friends.")

So women who enjoyed being entered in the seventies, whether by fingers or (even more taboo) sex toys, had to do so secretly. In some crowds, finger penetration was okay, but toys were considered gross representations of the phallically oriented patriarchy. Only the gentlest clitoral stroking was allowed, in addition to lots of hugging and cuddling and soft massage. (Ms. Behavior likes to imagine that there might also have been renegades who held dimly lit penetration parties, where the music had a throbbing, pulsating beat and the female bouncers at the door had huge hands.)

The teenage Ms. Behavior was not yet sexually active during this period, but she remembers the buzz of controversy and wishing she was having any sex at all, never mind being picky about what kind. Mostly she looked longingly at the women she knew were lesbians and grew mute while thinking about their sexual practices. "I'll do anything. Anything!" she cried into her pillow at night.

During this same period, Ms. Behavior's friend Josephine, the first lesbian she knew personally, went to the gynecologist and asked if her vaginal infection might be contagious to her lover. The doctor informed Josephine that it might be transmitted if she shared sex toys with her partner. Josephine had a fit, practically foaming at the mouth about the doctor's assumption that she would allow anything near her body that might even vaguely resemble a penis. Josephine was so loud and emphatic in her response that Ms. Behavior is sure that the gynecologist is now thoroughly convinced that Lesbians Do Not Use Sex Toys!

Over the years, especially in the mid-eighties, sex-positive groups began to emerge to combat judgment against things like penetration, s/m, and pornography. Some women began to admit publicly that they liked the feeling of something, anything, deep inside during sex, and risked their standing in the community by whipping out vibrators and dildos. A few particularly brave women even acknowledged that they didn't mind if their sex toys looked like penises as long as they were latex and didn't *act* like penises. Luckily, for those women who are squeamish about realistic representations of veins and testicles, some ultra-sensitive manufacturers have created sex toys that are very smooth, contoured, and nonpenislike, and even some that are designed to look like cuddly animals or other nonthreatening things.

Ms. Behavior's friend Tiffany, whose sexual consciousness developed beneath the giant thumb of the political dogma of the seventies, was thrilled when she started dating a sex goddess named Ophelia, who sported a huge dildo collection. Every night Tiffany called Ms. Behavior and whispered, "Oh my God. You just wouldn't believe what she had me do to her today. I tied her up. I held her down. I strapped it on. I felt *so* powerful. And *this* dildo was even *bigger* than last week's."

Ms. Behavior suspected that Tiffany made these disclosures for reasons of both excitement and confession. Tiffany had internalized the antipenetration creed to the point where she felt as if she were going against the rules of her religion. It was rebellion against her politically correct training that compelled her to confess, and it was this very same rejection of her penetration-free education that made her encounters with Ophelia and her huge, neon dildos so thrilling.

Since the rapture of penetration is twofold (i.e., doing it and/or being done to), Ms. Behavior got to hear about these adventures from both sides. As soon as Ms. Behavior would hang up with Tiffany, her phone would ring again, and she would hear Ophelia's excited voice. "Boy, that woman sure knows how to move her hips," she would say. "And you should see how *big* it was this time." (Any gay men who happen to be reading this section might be happy to know that size-queenism seems to be flowing over into the lesbian population.)

So now that we're practically into the third millennium and there are sex-toy catalogues and sex clubs just for lesbians, and videos teaching you *How to Find Your G-Spot with Dildos* and *How to Female Ejaculate,* who's gonna say you shouldn't explore the joys of penetration? Certainly not Ms. Behavior.

Ms. Behavior does offer a few words of caution, however. She urges you to look sensibly and realistically at the size of anything with which you want to become particularly intimate. Many a lesbian has been unhappy with a hurriedly purchased sex toy, which happens when her eyes are bigger than her . . . appetite.

Also, you must be cautious about purchasing something too small. Ms. Behavior's friend Nichole tried to buy a sensible-looking dildo that was only a little larger than her middle finger. The salesperson looked at her oddly and then asked her if she was aware that it was not actually a dildo but a butt plug. Nichole was too embarrassed to admit that she had not known, so she said a butt plug was exactly what she was looking for, thank you, and took it home with her.

Ms. Behavior also recommends that you beware of the emotions you can transfer onto a sex toy, especially if you name it. Tiffany was devastated when, after ending her relationship with Ophelia, she received a box full of little latex bits in the mail. Tiffany knew it was Diana, the dildo that she and Ophelia had come to love the most. She felt crushed by this gesture, because she knew that it was Ophelia's way of telling her that she never wanted to speak with her again.

It must be someone's grandmother that Ms. Behavior is channeling when she gets the uncontrollable desire to warn you not to use an electic vibrator after you've just emerged from the shower, and to clean your sex toys carefully if you share them. Be kind to your toys and they will be kind to you.

Anyway, Ms. Behavior is glad to resolve this penetration issue once and for all. Although there are always people who will want to judge what you do or don't do in bed, you can tell them to bug off. They are probably just jealous because they are not having any sex at all, so they want to limit the joyful expression of your desire and passion too. Never mind what they say — go for it. Ms. Behavior thinks penetration can be beautiful if you are open to it.

Part Six

FALLING IN LOVE
& STAYING
IN LOVE

Chapter Thirty-Seven

✦ ✦ ✦

HOW TO MEET THE PERSON OF YOUR DREAMS AND FALL IN LOVE

How many people have told you that if you want to meet someone and fall in love, it will "just happen" if you go on with the ordinary business of your life? Ms. Behavior appreciates such optimism, but is wise enough (or at least old enough) to know that this is not the whole picture. Think of the Buddhist notion of holding two opposing things, one in each hand, simultaneously; one represents going on with your life without thinking about falling in love, the other represents preparation for the magical moment when you do. Such spiritual gymnastics are not necessary for casual dating, but to be truly ready for love, Ms. Behavior believes, you must achieve two states that may seem contradictory: a Zenlike meditative bliss which keeps you happy in the moment and the intense preparedness of a Boy Scout.

Some of the groundwork you need to do is physical, and the rest is emotional. The type of preparation you should undertake depends on how you want to present yourself when you meet someone. Imagine that you will meet someone this afternoon in the supermarket. You are squeezing a kiwi, and the person of your dreams is squeezing a kiwi next to you. You can tell by the tender caress of the fruit that this person is someone whose sweet touch you would like to awaken with each morning.

You are desperate to talk to him or her and might even be ready to propose marriage or at least a long honeymoon, but you are too self-conscious, because you know you haven't (a) shaved or waxed your legs (usually applies to women); (b) shaved or waxed your mustache (applies to either gender); (c) washed the dirty dishes in your sink, which you worry will be revealed when you lose control and invite this person back to your apartment despite your better judgment; (d) said your morning prayers to the Goddess of Codependency, which you know are a must before plunging into even the most rudimentary infatuation.

What do you do, in light of your totally unprepared state? You give this perfect person one last, lingering glance and move on to the razor-blade aisle, where you make a quick purchase. Then you spend the rest of the day clutching your Gillette Sensor to your chest with your shades drawn, burning black candles and listening to Morrissey.

Building your emotional musculature for the crucial moment of meeting your ideal lover is just as important as preparing physically (which includes grooming, working out, and lots of moisturizing). There is nothing that potentially batters your self-esteem more than a new relationship, so being ready for falling in love involves pumping it up emotionally. It helps to think of this as intentionally getting fat in preparation for a long fast.

The unimaginative try to achieve this heightened self-esteem by burning incense and sitting naked in front of their full-length mirrors, reciting affirmations. Ms. Behavior's friend Jack admits to disrobing on a daily basis, looking lovingly at his own reflection, and saying, "I am a beautiful and loving child of God, no less than the stars in the sky. I am rich, virile, and tender. My hair is gorgeous and my skin blemish-free." Ms. Behavior knew it was wrong to laugh upon hearing his confession, but she laughed so hard that her seltzer came out her nose.

The un-embarrassing way to enhance your self-image is to become your own ideal lover. (Ms. Behavior is now channeling Dr. Joyce Brothers.) Ms. Behavior acknowledges the limitations of this method; you obviously won't be able to dive like Greg Louganis just because you admire his body, and you should not necessarily have your breasts enlarged just because you love Dolly. If, however, you are attracted to fit, spiritual people who read a lot, you might start working out, meditating, and spending your free time at the library instead of lying on the couch eating high-fat popcorn and bemoaning your fate at being single. This method will not only improve your self-esteem; it will also get you out of your house so that you can meet people, as well as give you something to talk about other than what happened on the most recent *Mary Tyler Moore* rerun.

You know why this self-strengthening is necessary: Once you go beyond ordinary dating and fall in love, you lose your center and become a jiggly, gelatinous cling-on. That warm, liquid feeling in your lover's presence becomes a drug that both awakens you and gives you a sensation of sleepy calm. Your sense of self begins to erode and you have to look in the mirror all the time to remember who you are. You shed your own interests and become obsessed with the things that intrigue your lover, even if his bizarre hobbies include sixteenth-century archaeology, collections of Snoopy dolls, and the care and breeding of iguanas.

You forget to return your friends' phone calls, and your family becomes a distant memory. You are late for work at least twice a week, and when your boss yells at you, you just smile. The heap of laundry in your bedroom is shoulder high, with your whites and colors happily commingling. Your therapist gets exasperated with your faraway look and tells you that she hates seeing people who are in love because they are rendered deaf and silly by their own passion.

At first this losing yourself feels wonderful; it's an emotional high like no other. Merging with another person, body and soul, feels like a giant psychic orgasm. But soon you realize that your life has slipped away, that you don't even remember what used to interest you. Beneath your new collection of Snoopy dolls and reptiles are small clues about what your life used to be like, and like a victim of amnesia, you try to piece them together. Your memory of self has been sucked into the black hole of obsessive love.

Ms. Behavior cannot bear to see this happen to you. She has witnessed too many body snatchings and cannot stand to see even one more. And besides, she wants your body and mind to be fertile ground upon which blissful, radiant love can do its carefree dance.

All Ms. Behavior has ever wanted is your happiness. It is from this place of guidance within that she will now tell you what you need to do to prepare for falling in love:

Floss and brush your teeth.
Use high-quality skin-care products.
Buy new sheets and fabulously sexy underwear.
Spend a lot of time cultivating your hobbies and friends.
Ride your bicycle.
Plant things in your garden.
Go to therapy and discuss your mother and your father, over and over again.
Be nice to your pets.
Visit your grandparents.
Avoid people who are deeply cynical.
Burn pretty candles.
Come out to everyone you know.
Keep fresh flowers in a vase in your living room.

Take your vitamins.
Meditate.
Recycle.

Once you have done all of this, you will be ready to fall in love. Also, you will be pretty damn appealing. In fact, if you follow through on all of these suggestions and you're female, send Ms. Behavior your phone number. She would like to have a word with you.

Chapter Thirty-Eight

✦ ✦ ✦

IS IT JUST INFATUATION OR IS IT REALLY LOVE?

Dear Ms. Behavior:

I met a fabulous *man recently and instantly felt like I was in love with him, even though I barely know him. I'm not sure whether he knows I exist or not, so it is causing me some pain. My friends tell me that what I am feeling is not love but merely obsession. How can you tell the difference? Either way, I remain*

— Smitten

Dear Smitten:

Ms. Behavior is happy to provide you with the lowdown on love versus obsession, although she is too embarrassed to disclose her own ratio of these experiences.

When you are in love, images of your own physiology fill your mind. You might, for example, feel like a new compartment in your heart has opened, or you might visualize your chest expanding to make room for the swelling of your new feelings.

When you are obsessed, you cannot keep your feelings to yourself. You tell everyone you know how you are feeling, how happy you are, how perfect your new lover is. You talk about how smooth his feet are, the softness of his caress. But when you're in love, you don't find yourself endlessly babbling to your friends about your new lover; thinking of your beloved is a little private treat, a secret you savor. You do not share. He is the warm loaf of bread you eat under the covers, the stolen cup of cocoa you drink when no one is around.

True love causes you to get oddly weepy over small things and fills you with bittersweet feelings that can make you cry at any moment, even during sex. Being in love is like being really premenstrual, even if you're a man. You become overly drippy and somewhat disgusting to be around, especially to your deeply cynical friends, who claim to want you to be happy but are really invested in having you remain as miserable as they are. When you are in love, your friends are overcome with jealousy, and they torture you. They imitate the vacant look on your face and try to make you feel uncool.

When you are obsessed, you think of the object of your desire throughout the whole day. When you wake up in the morning, you envision what she looks like awakening. You imagine her brushing her teeth, although you try not to picture her spitting. You wonder what she eats for breakfast and try to eat the same thing so that somehow you will be magically linked. When you get to work, you call her answering machine to listen to the sound of her voice. You love the way she says her name and explains that she can't come to the phone right now. You always wonder, in any given moment, if she is thinking of you.

On an especially obsessive day, you drive by her house, trying to see in the windows. You become curious about her ex-lovers and try to run into them. When you do meet them, you decide that they are too butch or too femme or too porcine and that you are much cuter. You can't eat a thing for two weeks and then you eat everything in sight, even some frozen hot-dog buns that are covered with a two-inch layer of ice. You lie in bed in your flannel pajamas, clutching your pillow, wondering what she is wearing. You wonder if she is lying in bed thinking about you.

Your friends start to avoid you, or at least start to change the subject a lot. You wonder what you did before you met her, because you cannot imagine what your life would be like without her. You pull out a dusty old journal and start writing again, mostly adolescent musings about pain and longing and unrequited love, mixed in with the occasional sexual fantasy.

You get a dramatic haircut. You listen to wrist-slashing music about love and feel that the songs were written for you. You start wearing makeup again and ordering sexy new underwear from catalogues. You close your eyes and envision kissing her.

When your obsession gets really bad, at its peak, you start asking yourself philosophical questions. You think about the nature of love versus lust or obsession, and you even start writing to advice columnists, looking for answers. You poor thing. Ms. Behavior trusts you will be out of your misery soon enough.

Chapter Thirty-Nine

✦ ✦ ✦

LONG-DISTANCE
ROMANCE VS.
MOVING IN

*I*f you ever have a choice between dating the boy or girl next door and someone who lives far away, Ms. Behavior would always suggest going for the long-distance lover. Distant love allows you to dress in black turtlenecks and look gaunt and tragic. You can complain about the ache in your heart and write anguished poetry about separation and loss. You can go back to smoking cigarettes, drinking coffee, and watching all-night TV; your friends will regard you as a tortured romantic soul. The best part about long-distance romance is that it has much of the dramatic appeal of unrequited passion or a married lover, without the angst.

Besides, what better way is there to fan the flames of romance than to do it from another state, where you don't have to deal with the daily realities that make relationships hard? Hundreds or thousands of miles allow for intense intimacy and frenzied lovemaking when you and your lover are together, and also permit time for each of you to reassemble your lives while you are apart.

After each love-filled, erotic weekend, you get to wash your sticky sheets, clean your apartment, pay your bills, and see your friends. This helps you to gain some semblance of a real life, apart from the delicious swelling of all-consuming love. Missing someone inspires you to send flowers and to express tender sentiments that would be extinguished much sooner with daily contact. What thrill could be greater than the sweet anticipation of seeing your lover after weeks of longing, then running toward each other at the airport and finally collapsing into each other's arms?

It's not just that absence makes the heart grow fonder; time also filters out all of your lover's weird habits, so that you remember only his tender gestures and witty comments. Once you are alone, pining for your lover, you forget that each morning he coughs and spits phlegm into the sink, or that she leaves hundreds of long auburn hairs clogging your shower drain. You don't think about his deadly indecisiveness or about her struggle to control all your weekend plans.

This combination of selective amnesia and pumped-up fantasy makes you happy. You lie in bed alone thinking about his soft skin or her supple buttocks, and you count the days until your reunion. You imagine her curled behind you, the sweet smell of her hair close to your face, filling your nostrils. You can practically feel his beard against your neck when he leans over to kiss you goodnight. A delicious longing fills you as you drift off to sleep, dreaming of your lover's body wrapped around yours, warming your bed.

Still, not everyone is lucky enough to find a lover who lives far away. If you and your lover lack the advantage of living in separate cities, Ms. Behavior recommends that you at least maintain separate living quarters for as long as possible. Long-distance relationships work because they provide boundaries that prevent you from having to deal with the merging problem that erodes so many live-in unions. (See more about this in the Lesbian Bed Death chapter.) The longer you maintain a separate identity, the less you will feel like some kind of paramecium with permeable cell walls who is being consumed by another single-cell organism.

After a brief period of romantic dating from afar, your lover will probably start begging you to move in with him. Your excuses about not wanting to relocate will not work for long, because after a while he will offer to leave his job and his life to be with you. But even if you love his taste in furniture, bedding, and dishes, Ms. Behavior urges you to think about this very carefully before agreeing.

Although living together can feel exciting and intimate at first, it can weld you together like a pair of Siamese twins. This unification initially feels sweet; you want nothing more than to absorb your lover and to become one with him. Your fusion fills that empty space inside you, making you happier than Prozac ever did.

You love the feeling of pressing your chest to hers, how it opens up your heart. You want to watch him sleep, to kiss him as he awakens each morning, to bring him toast and eggs in bed. You can tell that she is the woman with whom you want to watch videos every night, the person whose lingerie you want hanging over your shower rod each day, the one whose oversized shoes you want to trip over.

Soon, however, your toothbrushes and laundry are commingling and you are wearing each other's clothing and cologne. You hang out with each other's friends, and you adopt each other's expressions, mannerisms, and voices until your own parents can't tell you apart on the phone. Once you begin to walk and dress alike, the decline quickens. After a while, you find yourself saying, "Honey, is that you or me in this photograph?"

At first this merging is amusing, but soon you realize that you feel more like siblings than lovers. By the time that happens, even Ms. Behavior could not possibly save you: Your relationship is doomed to become sexless.

Ms. Behavior realizes that her well-intentioned admonitions are likely to go unheeded when lust or romance enters the picture. Many readers in the throes of hot passion will rush to move in together in spite of Ms. Behavior's elaborate warning.

If you do decide to combine domiciles, be sure to maintain your individual interests, which may help to keep you from blending into one big blob o' homo. Don't give up your Monday night mandolin classes in order to stay at home and watch *Murphy Brown* together, and do not pretend to be fascinated with topiary design just to be closer to your lover. The more you do to expand and enliven your own pursuits, the less likely it is that you will have to write desperate letters to advice columnists about your miserable existence with your lover.

It helps to fight about real things on occasion, instead of just bickering about boring domestic matters. Real conflict can keep passion burning longer, especially if you get mad enough to pin your lover down from time to time, in an attempt to achieve top-dog status.

For now, until such time as you move all of your possessions in with your lover's and join the ranks of cohabiting homosexuals, be sure to enjoy the sound of your lover's zipper moving along its track as he prepares to leave. The zipper on his suitcase, that is.

Chapter Forty

✦ ✦ ✦

CHOOSING YOUR
ANNIVERSARY DATE

Gay men lead lives of enviable simplicity. Unlike lesbians, who frequently spend the first three years of their relationship trying to figure out their anniversary date, gay men have the gift of extraordinary clarity. While dykes struggle to decide whether to celebrate the day they met, their first date, their first sex act, or the date they fell in love, gay men generally do not have this dilemma, because all of these events took place on the same glorious day, leaving them with only one choice for an anniversary date. Lucky fags!

The stages of gay men's relationships are the same as those of lesbians: Infatuation and Sexual Enchantment, Sweet Comfort and Connection, Boredom, Infidelity (optional), and Breakup. But since gay men are on shorter cycles than lesbians in terms of the duration of their relationships, they are also on a shorter celebration schedule. This means that they often celebrate anniversaries monthly instead of annually, so that they can fit it all in.

Pardon Ms. Behavior for her presumptuousness if you happen to be a gay man who lives more like a dyke, or a lesbian whose relationships tend to be on an abbreviated cycle, like a fag's. If you have a resentment, let it flow. Ms. Behavior will be happy to read your indignant mail.

Anyway, if you are a normal lavender-blooded lesbian, Ms. Behavior suspects that you suffer from some specific dyke-defining characteristics, including a propensity for excessive negotiation. Once you find yourself uttering the L-word ("love," not "lesbian"), you and your girlfriend must succumb to the ritual of haggling over your anniversary date so that you know when to joyously celebrate your blessed union.

Such ceremonies, just like the celebration of solstices, are very beautiful and very lesbian; you had better get used to them if you are committed to being a dyke. Besides, in a year or two, when an occasional bit of domestic strife arises, it will be nice to have a day when you light candles, give each other romantic gifts, and exchange back rubs with scented oils. Avoid patchouli oil, however, unless you aspire for that I've-just-returned-from-a-wimmin's-music-festival odor. Once you go out in public, it will make women rush to peel off their shirts and dance in topless circles around you, which will embarrass you in social situations.

Ms. Behavior understands the difficulty that lesbians have in agreeing on an anniversary date. She has usually chosen the date of the first kiss, and if her lover hasn't agreed, she has tortured her into compliance. She has seen other couples, however, who start out engaged in mild discussion but end up throwing their collection of naked-woman mugs at each other in anger. What do you do if your lover wants the date to be the time your eyes met across the room at the Holly Near concert, but you want to celebrate the first time her tongue touched yours? Tickle or cajole her until she agrees. Or be the grownup and give in for once.

Try not to take it as a betrayal if your lover wants your anniversary to be the first day you had sex; it might mean that she just has intimacy issues. Do not write letters of complaint to Ms. Behavior saying, "My love is such a man. She wants our anniversary to commemorate the first day we did the nasty."

Remember that the date you are choosing is one of celebration, so your goal is to come to some sort of agreement instead of turning the discussion into a tofu-tossing argument. Some lesbians find that they need to celebrate two dates, because they cannot concur. This alternative is fine, but you must actually seem enthusiastic when celebrating the one that matters to your lover.

Ms. Behavior reminds you to select your anniversary date carefully, because the date you choose will be yours to keep "forever," unless you want to go through the ugly business of starting all over again, which would necessitate a breakup followed by a blissful reunion. Or, even worse, a breakup followed by meeting a new lover and having to go through the whole process all over again.

Think, before you choose, about what is most significant to you. If you're romantic, you can probably pinpoint the day you fell in love. Practical types will choose their first date, because it's easy to remember and they don't have to consider the emotional variables. If you're a very sexual lesbian, you might opt for the first time you made love or even the date of that incredible tantric orgasm that shook you all the way to your teeth.

In any case, if you and your lover cannot agree on an anniversary date, trouble lies ahead. If you find, say, that you are a romantic soul and your lover is practical, start saving money for couple's therapy: She's probably the type who will forget your anniversary anyway.

Chapter Forty-One

✦ ✦ ✦

HOW TO DEAL WITH
YOUR LOVER'S
PSYCHO FAMILY

When you first get involved in a relationship, your lover seems like he was made just for you, which makes it easy to forget that he has any sort of past. You overlook the fact that he was raised by a tribe of people who might share his cute aquiline nose or overbite as well as some of his finer and/or odder personality characteristics. You are not especially eager to meet these people, because you are too busy with your wild infatuation to care, and also because you don't want your fantasy to be crushed like an insect beneath the big clumsy foot of genetic reality.

Besides, your lover has a few worries of his own; he is scared to death that if you meet his family, you will not be amused by their quirks. What if you notice that his father's idiosyncracy about germs is really some type of wacko phobia, or if you think his mother's tendency toward garish decorating might be inheritable? If your lover does not exactly encourage this encounter, it is because he fears that you not only will decide never to move in with him but might also be inspired to catch the next 747 to Guadalajara.

You probably have an equally scary family that you'll have to bring out of hiding. Once you and your lover realize that neither of these frightening meetings can be postponed forever, go out and buy a couple of new outfits and get ready for your big adventure.

Your coping skills play a large part in determining what will happen. Ms. Behavior advises you to try to work for a peaceful, observant mood before you even leave your house. Buddhist chanting would probably help, or at least repeating a prayer over and over, like "Goddess, please help me not to reveal my violent temper. Ommmmm. Goddess, please help me not to argue politics or spill food on the host. Ommmmmm."

Once you have achieved this serene attitude, you will have the opportunity to assess your lover's family before deciding how to behave. Your calm stance will prevent you from reacting impulsively — by jumping out of a moving car on the way to a restaurant with them, for example — and you can gather up your energy if you do need to do anything dramatic, like pretending to have a heart attack between dinner and dessert so the welcome sound of an ambulance pulling into the parking lot will release you from any further horror. (Do not attempt to pretend to choke, because an overly enthusiastic restaurant employee with hero fantasies might attempt to give you an emergency tracheotomy.)

Personality assessment skills can only be developed over time, but Ms. Behavior is happy to offer some information about a few general types of family members. If you happen to recognize any of these, you will know just how to act.

Ms. Behavior warns you that if your lover's mother seems too sweet to be real, she probably is. Ms. Behavior once had a lover with a Sweet Mother, which is far more terrifying than it sounds. The Sweet Mother is the type who kisses you, welcomes you to the family, and tries to get you to call her Mom. Usually employed as a nursery school teacher or a librarian, she will bake your favorite cookies and include you in all the family events. Be aware, however, that she expects something in return, which is generally your compliance with her odd set of unspoken rules about pretending that nothing sexual or romantic is really happening between you and her child.

Ms. Behavior has found, for example, that kissing or fondling the Sweet Mother's child in even the subtlest manner will cause the veins on her neck to pop out and her face to turn red with fury. And if you dare to suggest to the Sweet Mother's friends that you are violating her innocent offspring, she will become fierce, a sharp-toothed lioness savagely protecting her little cub. She will also rip that chocolate-chip cookie right out of your mouth so fast that your lips will bleed.

But the Sweet Mother is easy compared to the Fusion Mother, the deadliest mommy in the animal kingdom. This mother so much resents your involvement with her progeny (for whom she unconsciously harbors romantic feelings) that there is no way you could ever prove yourself to be good enough for her child.

Ms. Behavior's friend Wendy dated a woman with a Fusion Mother, and she described the situation as a neat twist on the Oedipal complex: "Laura's mother wants to kill me and marry Laura. I am nothing but an obstacle to the fulfillment of her deepest desires." Wendy also lamented that Laura's mother had not yet scratched out her own eyes, but she hoped that that was forthcoming.

If you've ever had a lover with a Twisted Father (frequently married to the Sweet Mother), you will never forget him. "You're lucky to have a father-in-law like me," he says, "because I accept you for your aberrant behavior." His hobby is writing laudatory letters to people like Rush Limbaugh, Newt Gingrich, and Dan Quayle, whose responses are prominently displayed on the wall next to his deer antlers. He sends weekly newspaper clippings, addressed to the two of you, that tell stories of fathers who disown their children for being gay, and encloses a note reminding you both of your good fortune. Try not to visit unless he is on one of his weekend retreats with the NRA.

The Love-Child Father, in contrast, is no problem at all. He doesn't care whether his child shaves his head and wears magenta hip boots, and wouldn't notice if he joined a cult and danced naked down Main Street. This means he won't mind if you boff his son in his home, even if it's on the dining room table while he sits at the other end and eats his Cheerios.

The most embarrassing of all, though, are the We-Accept-You-Just-the-Way-You-Are Parents. You can tell them from any other kind because they are the ones who wear pink triangle emblems on their leather bomber jackets and spend most of their time at the library, gleaning newspaper clips on homosexuality. Ms. Behavior's friend Oogie was tortured by his lover's parents as a teenager. Oogie and his lover Ralph were awakened early one morning by Ralph's father, who informed them that the *Boston Globe* was there to take their picture. Oogie was too disoriented to object, so he and Ralph were photographed by the *Globe* at Ralph's father's request. The headline read, "Look, Mom and Dad, We're Gay." Oogie has never been so embarrassed in his entire gay life.

When you and your lover go to their house, the We-Accept-You-Just-the-Way-You-Are Parents welcome you profusely and offer you the use of their waterbed for the weekend. They try to smoke pot with you and expect you to engage in interpretive dance with them in their living room. Whatever you do, don't encourage them.

Parents are not the only characters in your lover's family drama; your lover's siblings can also provide you with hours of free entertainment. Beware, however, if your female lover has a Seductive Sister; she's a scary one, and you'll have to watch your back.

The Seductive Sister had one lesbian experience during her sophomore year at Sarah Lawrence (she's still pissed that she didn't go to Smith), and she's been dying to duplicate that fabulous moment ever since. She asks you coy questions about what lesbians do in bed (as if she doesn't know!) and talks incessantly about the erotic kissing in the dyke film of the moment. Her walls are covered with unsubtle lesbo art, and she has nude black-and-white photographs of some of her friends in "creative" poses hanging over her bed. When you are tired, she offers to rub your shoulders and feet. Be pleasant but firm as you say no. She will make it look as though you are doing something wrong, even though you are not.

Another dangerous sibling is the Butch Brother. If you're a woman in love with his sister, the Butch Brother will simultaneously flirt with you and treat you with disdain. He cannot believe that you would be more attracted to his sister than to him, and he will tease you and try to interest you in his bulging muscles. Treat him like a pesky dog. A rap on the nose with a newspaper will work if verbal discouragement does not.

If you're a man in love with his brother, the Butch Brother will totally ignore you. He both hopes and fears that you will find him attractive and is afraid of what that would mean about him, so he runs to the gym on the day you visit and works up a good manly sweat. You can tell a Butch Brother from one who is not because the real thing won't shower when he comes home from the gym. He doesn't realize, however, that unconsciously he is doing that to attract you with his pheromones.

As you prepare for your first visit to your lover's family, try not to be distracted by your worries of how they will receive you. Just attempt to be as normal as possible, and try to get rid of the expression on your face that indicates you think you are attending a wake. You may wonder what to take the first time you visit; Ms. Behavior believes that you can never go wrong with a fruitcake.

Chapter Forty-Two

✦　✦　✦

FANTASIZING ABOUT

SOMEONE ELSE

*E*ven if you are a good and beautiful person, at some point during your relationship with your lover you will find yourself noticing someone else. Although you've been safely ensconced in your warm love nest and have never intended to stray, eventually you meet someone cute and begin to see this person frequently, perhaps at work or your health club or when you walk your dog. It starts out as a tiny, innocent thrill that makes you smile. Over time, however, this little flutter may turn into a full-blown gigantic attraction that causes mega-hot bare-skin fantasies which really shake you up.

If you run into the Object of Your Fantasy every time you go to the Xerox machine and then spend the rest of the day imagining him lying naked on the beach, a lovely pool of perspiration gathered in the hollow between his pecs, this will eventually cause you a lot of anguish. You might also drool all over your work reports and crush them between your sweaty palms while you stand there stammering. (Asking your secretary to do your photocopying will offer only minimal relief, because you are sure to run into your fantasy babe during your lunch break or, worse, in the bathroom.)

You know it's bad when you start thinking about this person even when you don't see him, fantasizing about what it might be like to press your mouth against his. As the days pass, your imaginings grow, and you think about slowly undressing him, sliding your hand beneath his shirt, over his hard stomach and chest. You know you are in trouble when your fantasies progress the way a relationship does: Soon you go beyond mere sex and envision reading the Sunday *Times* in bed. You even romanticize the idea of doing dishes with him. By the time the door to your imagination opens this far, you might as well rip it off the hinges. You are doomed.

Even Ms. Behavior, who is usually fairly devoted, has found that her eyes occasionally wander (and sometimes even cross). Luckily, Ms. Behavior has mostly been attracted to people who have been inaccessible for one reason or another, a fact that has kept her safe from her own lasciviousness. (The psychobabbically oriented might suggest that perhaps Ms. Behavior desires only people who are harmless in their unavailability.) Otherwise, she probably would have appeared on *Geraldo* by now, with a caption under her face reading "Unfaithful Lesbian Suffers from Uncontrollable Fantasies."

Fantasizing can be a harmless diversion which can boost your self-esteem and make you feel attractive. A little flirting can be good for hours of innocent entertainment, as long as you make it clear to the Object of Your Fantasy that you aren't really available. But if this flirting takes all of your attention away from your primary relationship, your lover will eventually notice your withdrawal and become pissy about it. If you let the attraction progress far enough, you and your lover will bicker all the time, and you will end up in the worst kind of trouble there is: The Dreaded Couple's Therapy. *Yikes!*

How do you tell when you are stepping over the line into the dangerous part of fantasizing? You must be very careful to pay attention to the early warning signs. If you ignore these, you may end up betraying your sweet, trusting lover. And then won't you feel like scum?

You know you've got it really bad when all the horribly mushy songs on the radio remind you of the OYF (Object of Your Fantasy). You are in a hellish predicament if Partridge Family hits, like "I Think I Love You," bring tears to your eyes. Ms. Behavior can envision you driving around in your car, singing "Somewhere (There's a Place for Us)" at the top of your lungs. Even the Carpenters make you feel sappy inside, and you find yourself wondering if your secret fantasy person also thinks of you when she hears "Close to You" on the radio. Is this pathetic, or what?

Now when you sit across the dinner table and look at your lover, he is eclipsed by the image of the other man. You chew your food slowly, trying to see only your lover's face, but you have to close your eyes because you see halos and shadows of your secret crush and feel as if you might be blinded by the pressure coming from behind your eyes. Ohhhhhhhh. This is getting painful.

You are shopping for your lover's Valentine's Day present, and you keep tripping across things the OYF would like. Would it really be so bad to give him a present? What if you pretend your gesture of affection and desire is just a joke? You send a dozen roses, but you don't sign the card. You don't want to tell him the flowers are from you, but you hope he figures it out. You are so confused.

It has happened to Ms. Behavior on more than one occasion. When Ms. Behavior's lover grabs her hand in the movies, she shudders for a moment, imagining it is Rhonda, her scuba-diving instructor. Ms. Behavior barely watches the movie, because she is consumed with wishing she could sit in a darkened theater with Rhonda and feel Rhonda's fingers brushing against hers in the oily popcorn bucket.

Do not under any circumstances work out with the person to whom you are attracted, because you will be tortured by the sight of his clothing pressing lightly against his hard body. You will stand behind him and inhale the pungent fragrance of his sweat, wishing you could rub it all over your body. Without thinking about it, you will lightly touch the wet spot on his back, pleased to feel his stickiness through his shirt. Ay caramba.

If you invest enough time in being in places you should not be, the inevitable happens: The other woman confesses her attraction to you, and you are in *big* trouble. What started out as a fantasy now has the potential to become real. If she is creative in her expression of desire for you, it may take superhuman willpower to resist being ensnared by her pulsating libido.

Although it seems nearly impossible, it would be best to try to turn away from this potential passion, because it can take over like a brushfire. In one moment it is a tiny spark, and in the next you have burned down not just your own house but your entire neighborhood.

Whatever you do, do not allow the OYF to give you a massage. He will wait for that moment of tension when he sees you reaching for your neck, and he will gently replace your hands with his own firm ones. Ahhhhh. His touch feels so strong and yet so tender. Now that his hands have touched your neck, what harm would there be in progressing to your shoulders? Your back? Your buttocks? *Stop! Oh my God, STOP!!*

Do not listen if she begins to talk about her physical reaction to your presence. She will start out describing delicate images, like the way you make her heart flutter, the way you make her mouth open with desire and anticipation. Soon she will progress to the swelling in her chest. (As soon as she says the word "swelling," it's all over.) The next thing you know, you will get a piece of her cotton nightgown in the mail. You will hold it close to your face, imagining her scent. Suddenly, you realize it *is* covered with her scent, but it is not the smell of her moisturizer or deodorant. It is a much more personal sort of scent. Ay-yi-yi!

Can you feel the buildup? Can you tell how unsafe it is to live in the world with all of these possibilities knocking at your door, trying to lure you from the safety of your relationship?

Stay at home. Leave your house only to buy lots of Happy Meals, fried chicken, and Sara Lee crumb cakes, in an attempt to gain forty pounds quickly. Watch cartoons and sitcoms that dull your mind. Tell your friends that you need adult supervision. Ask your lover to take you on vacation. But do not — Ms. Behavior repeats, do *not* — kiss the Object of Your Fantasy.

Perhaps no one has told you, but kissing is both the road to heaven and the gateway to hell. If you are free to kiss and fall in love, than Ms. Behavior offers her sincere blessing and a package of breath mints. If you are not, especially if it is for reasons of being in another relationship, then she can only advise you to keep your tongue in your own mouth. Ms. Behavior cannot even report some of the scary places that "just kissing" has led some of her friends.

Once you reach this point, your life becomes very complicated. You are afraid to fall asleep for fear of what you might say when you are not conscious. When you have sex with your lover, you keep your eyes open the whole time so you don't accidentally moan the wrong name.

Your only chance for salvation now is to try to muster as much reality as you can. Envision yourself living with the OYF two years from now, when the sheen has worn off your attraction. Imagine that your infatuation, like the roses you sent for Valentine's Day, has begun to droop and lose color. Focus on the things that you think could potentially annoy you, and allow them to grow a thousandfold in your mind. Envision how you might feel after a year or two about his endearing habits of talking to his mangy little chihuahuas in a high-pitched voice and washing their food bowls with the kitchen sponge. Try to remember that his incredible stubbornness will no longer be cute once he turns it on you. And that his inability to make a decision, which seems funny now, will make you want to plunge a ginsu knife into him someday.

Think of all these things and then look at your quirky current lover, lying in bed next to you. The one whose faults are already predictable and annoyingly familiar, the one who drives you crazy. If you look at him while he sleeps, you will remember the innocence you once saw, how perfect he once seemed. Then you will be flooded with the memory of your fantasy about him, how much joy you anticipated in his presence, how convinced you were that he was the one. So you settle comfortably into his arms and close your eyes. You gratefully accept this moment of peace.

But you know as well as Ms. Behavior does that in the darkest part of the night, your fantasy love will steal his way into your bed and nuzzle his sweet face and body into your waiting embrace. As you fall asleep, you don't know whose voice it is, but you keep hearing the words, "This is the one."

Chapter Forty-Three

✦ ✦ ✦

LESBIAN BED DEATH:
REAL OR IMAGINED?

*P*lease, please don't ever wear white sweat socks to bed. Don't leave the bathroom door open while you are squeezing your zits, and don't pee while your lover is watching. Don't wear each other's clothes and hang out with each other's friends and develop all the same tastes and political ideologies. Ms. Behavior is trying to help you, okay? She believes that if you start early enough in your relationship, it might just be possible to prevent Lesbian Bed Death.

Ms. Behavior would like to be able to say that Lesbian Bed Death is not a real phenomenon, that it is a nasty rumor started by heterosexuals, designed to make lesbians look matronly and unsexy. She would like to say it absolutely doesn't exist.

But alas, Ms. Behavior has found too little evidence that lesbians in long-term relationships still have frequent and/or passionate sex to dispel this notion. So if you are part of a long-term (more than five years) lesbian couple and you are still really hot for each other and making love all the time, please write to Ms. Behavior and let her know so that she can correct this matter in her next book. She longs to be able to tell the world about you and your tender but gymnastically gifted lovemaking. And she needs more information on how to keep that heart-flame burning.

Without your help, Ms. Behavior might be forced to do a Lesbian Bed Death Telethon, which would be pathetic and publicly humiliating to us all. (Instead of sending money, viewers would send donations of sexy lingerie and videos called *Dykes Who Do It in the Front Seat* or *Lezzie Passion: Tie Me Up, Tie Me Down, Part II.*)

If it hasn't happened yet, you may think Lesbian Bed Death has nothing to do with you. You feel pity for those poor sexless dykes who have encountered this fate, but you feel certain that this will never occur in your relationship, because you and your lover are just *so* attracted to each other.

Unfortunately, Ms. Behavior is here to tell you that you need not be so smug, young lesbian; without the proper precautions, LBD can happen to anyone, even you. (Ms. Behavior would like to say that it has never happened in any of her relationships, but she knows she would go straight to hell for a lie of that magnitude. Also, she has too many ex-lovers who would testify in a court of law about all the nights they spent cuddling or holding hands with Ms. Behavior, united in prayer for a sexual feeling to emerge.)

Ms. Behavior knows that life is full of people who want to terrorize you with possibilities that will never come to pass: Don't stick your tongue out or your face will freeze like that. Don't talk to strangers or you'll be abducted. Don't play with scissors or you'll lose an eye. Just as you continued to play with matches even though your mother told you not to, you continue to tempt the Goddess of Eros by eating dinner in front of the TV while watching the football game. When your lover tries to talk to you, you just chew harder, grunt, and turn up the volume. If this is the beginning of your relationship and things still feel torrid, you can't imagine that one little football game will make a difference. Ms. Behavior would like to suggest, however, that there are some things you just have to take on faith, the same way you brush (and, she hopes, floss) your teeth even though you have no proof that they would all fall out if you didn't.

So here are some of Ms. Behavior's suggestions for the prevention of Lesbian Bed Death:

1. Do not wear flannel pajamas to bed unless the temperature falls below zero.

2. Do not go to bed with your hair wrapped in a sock.

3. Sleep naked sometimes, so that your skin can touch your lover's skin, but don't sleep naked every night, or the effect will be lost.

4. Every few months, wear a nurse's uniform or a cowboy outfit to bed.

5. Spend some time kissing each other passionately without expecting to make love.

6. Do not tell your lover the entire contents of your psychotherapy session while lying in bed.

7. If you must clip your toenails in front of your lover, don't leave the clippings in a little pile next to the bed.

8. When you talk about sex with your lover, try not to start the discussion with "You know what really bothers me?"

9. Don't fight in the bedroom, unless you're planning to turn it into a tie-me-up fight.

10. Do not lean down in your lover's general direction, sniff the air, and say, "Hmmm. Did you shower today?"

Ms. Behavior will not give you a list of tired suggestions on how to keep love alive by eating candlelit dinners together, going on theater dates, and buying each other roses. She also will not offer advice about putting a bag over your lover's head for the evening and pretending that she is someone new. For that kind of advice you can read *Cosmo* and just switch the gender.

Unlike lesbian author JoAnn Loulan, Ms. Behavior will not suggest that you slip your fingers inside your lover's underwear under the table at a restaurant. If, however, you choose to do so, Ms. Behavior hopes to be sitting at the next table so she can watch.

Straight couples sometimes suffer from LBD, but they don't know it. They call it the seven-year itch and sometimes live in a long-term sexless marriage, just like lesbians do. Or else they have affairs and/or get divorced, just like lesbians do.

Gay men, however, rarely stay together long enough to develop bed death, or they engage in activities that effectively stave it off. That occasional safe and anonymous tumble in the bushes that some men enjoy probably helps. And why, if not to fight off dullness, would gay men devote all of their time, money, and energy to redecorating every few weeks? Perhaps if lesbians would give up their plaid sofas and natural wood furniture and occasionally buy some stylish new things, it would awaken some of that stagnant energy. Ms. Behavior admits that consumerism is not a permanent solution, but it might work for a while. Compulsively purchasing new things is often about seeking emotional renewal, but most people don't realize that until they run out of things to buy.

Ms. Behavior's friend Tiffany insists that the chief cause of Lesbian Bed Death is disapproval of vibrators. Tiffany has a vibrator fetish, so Ms. Behavior is not sure she is objective. But just in case she is right, Ms. Behavior will say that if your sex life needs a new charge, you might go to the sex toy store and pick up something new.

Try to remember not to cuddle too much with your lover. Cuddling and holding hands can be a substitute for expressing energy in a more sexual way. When you are lying in bed with your lover, waiting for desire to take over, resist the temptation just to hold her all the time or to link your pinkies platonically. As you lie there looking into her eyes, you can make this into a sort of rhythmic reminder chant: "This woman is not my sister. This woman is not my friend. This woman is my lover. I desperately want to make love with her." Do this over and over again in your mind. Try not to chant out loud or your lover might either (a) be insulted or (b) call the psychiatric hospital and have you taken away.

Ms. Behavior suggests that you and your lover limit snacking in front of the TV to special occasions, unless you are prepared to love and accept each other's bodies even if they change dramatically. Most lesbians gain at least twenty-five pounds the first year they live together and add six or seven pounds each subsequent year; unless you both limit your Yodel intake, you may have to get used to a much more expansive version of the woman you love. Also, you might consider placing a strong wooden board beneath your mattress for support, because between the two of you, that could be one hundred extra sapphic pounds.

Ms. Behavior also consulted her friend Lynda, who refers to herself as the Dr. Kevorkian of Lesbian Bed Death. Lynda, who has never experienced passion lasting longer than a single solstice (ninety days) was able to offer suggestions only on how to cause LBD, not on how to prevent it. (Lynda is such an expert at killing sexual relationships that she cannot even reverse the process mentally in order to imagine deflecting LBD.) So here are the good doctor's suggestions for enhancing the effects of LBD.

1. Keep a TV in the bedroom and have it on at all times.

2. Let your big, smelly, drooly pets sleep in the bed with you, preferably between you.

3. Answer the phone whenever it rings, no matter what you might be doing or thinking about doing.

4. Keep a list of household projects near the bed and discuss the deck you want to build or what sort of bathroom sink you need to buy whenever things seem like they might turn amorous.

5. Eat a big bean burrito every night just before bed.

6. Work out at the gym and do not shower when you get home. (Ms. Behavior believes this particular suggestion could go either way, because some people like that hot, sweaty thang.)

7. Try to get your mother to call while you are making love. Turn up the volume on the answering machine so that you can listen to her voice.

8. Curl up next to your lover in bed and start talking about your ex-lovers.

When women really love each other but lose their sexual interest, they will do nearly anything to feel that wave of passion again. Prevention is key, because once LBD actually happens, it can be difficult to reverse. Ms. Behavior believes that resurrection is possible in some cases, however, and hopes you will share your experience with her. If you do find a way to heal a relationship that has already entered the cadaverous zone, please let Ms. Behavior know; she would love nothing more than to help spread the good news to lustful lesbians around the globe.

Ms. Behavior would also be happy to help you market the cure for this deadly malady, and she would split the proceeds with you. But only because she knows in her heart that she would be offering a valuable human service.

✦ ✦ ✦

Dear Ms. Behavior:

I have often wondered as I read your column whether I am doomed to a life of perpetual angst and misery with regards to my love relationships. I am not sure why I am asking you, because sometimes you seem just as grim as I. But tell me, Ms. Behavior, what hope is there for the likes of us?

— Doomed

Dear Doomed:

Ms. Behavior loves to tackle an existential challenge. While she is generally at one with God and goodness, she is also occasionally at one with the blackness of the universe. Such voices of good and evil emanate not from her but through her.

Ms. Behavior personally believes that it is possible for every person to cultivate love and beauty in his or her life and each person's Goddess-given right to experience such blessings fully. While Ms. Behavior considers it her duty to issue warnings about the potential pitfalls of relationships, she wishes her readers only happiness and fulfillment.

Although it may seem harsh when she suggests that you dump the dolt you are dating, it is often because Ms. Behavior has a vision of the bliss awaiting you around the corner. If you awaken to your own potential for everlasting love, it will stir and grow within you. Ms. Behavior further suggests that if you can see only grimness in the words of her columns, perhaps your eyes are blind to the ethereal beauty that pulsates through all matter and experience.

Besides, who asked you?

Chapter Forty-Four

✦ ✦ ✦

HAPPILY EVER
AFTER: WEDDINGS
AND COMMITMENT
CEREMONIES*

Think back to childhood, when you played with your bridal
Barbie, brushing her luxurious blond hair and walking her
down the aisle. She was the most radiant of your dolls, the one you
played with most. You sometimes ripped her limbs off in annoyance,
though, because you wanted her to marry Skipper (or Ken to marry
G.I. Joe) and you hadn't yet heard of commitment ceremonies.

Now that the wedding you orchestrate may be your own, Ms.
Behavior hopes that the reason for your ceremony is a tender expression of love. She hopes your wedding day is one you will always
remember as a joyful celebration of your union.

But perhaps you are headed for matrimony because you are hop-

---

*Warning: This is the chapter where Ms. Behavior turns sentimental.

ing to grab up enough cash for a down payment on a house or for new appliances. Don't gasp and hold your hand over your heart; it's a crude reason to get married, but straight people have been doing it for centuries, so please feel free at least to acknowledge the greedy impulse if you have it. You will feel better if you confess.

Maybe you plan to walk down the aisle to avenge the lifetime of hell your right-wing fan-of-Rush-Limbaugh parents have put you through. You fantasize about inviting the press so that you can send the newspaper clipping to all of their sanctimonious friends from church and the bridge club, including the photo of you and your lover kissing when you are pronounced husband and husband. If you dig deep to examine your soul and find that shocking your relatives is truly the motivation for your commitment ceremony, a little extra therapy is in order, because the brat within is running the show.

Perhaps you think a ceremony might finally convince your lover's ex-lover to take the hint and go away. Forget it. Your lover's marital status will only pose a more interesting challenge to her interloping ex, who will become even more persistent. Ms. Behavior has seen some of these obsessive ex-lovers and it would take a lot more than one silly little wedding to pry their claws from your lover's flesh.

If you're a gay man or lesbian with strong political convictions, you may decide to get married as a matter of principle, as a means of moving toward the legal and financial privileges that straight people enjoy as well as societal acceptance of your union. Ms. Behavior might be channeling her grandmother again, but she thinks a marriage based primarily on political beliefs is ultimately a sad thing, if not combined with affection and love. Your politics will not get you through the stressful times, when you want to just bang your lover on the head. Bang, bang, bang. Nor will you get to experience the delightful flutter of passion and intensity that your friends who are in love feel. Ultimately you will just become bitter and walk around with a sour look on your face, and no one will invite you to parties.

Don't get Ms. Behavior wrong; she wants anyone who wishes to wed to be able to do so, and she wants to be there too, throwing rice (or, if forced, the more politically correct birdseed). It's just that she wants love to be the guiding force in your decison to marry.

Ms. Behavior's mushiness about weddings may come as a surprise, because she has occasionally expressed cynical views, but she clearly has a sweet spot for matters of romance. Ms. Behavior truly hopes your commitment ceremony happens for one reason only: because you and your lover want to express and celebrate your eternal love and devotion.

Please do not throw gum at Ms. Behavior's hair and laugh at her sentimentality. It is how she feels. And if she ever decides to get married, she hopes it will be for this reason.

Now Ms. Behavior will reveal the questions she is asked most frequently about gay and lesbian marriage.

Question: *Where should I propose?*

Ms. Behavior's answer: Anywhere you have the impulse. But if you propose in bed, please make sure that you really mean it, that it does not just happen during a moment of pleasure or gratitude.

Question (usually asked by lesbians): *Should we invite our ex-lovers to our wedding?*

Ms. Behavior's answer: If your motivation is clear (i.e., you are inviting them because you want them to participate in your joyous day, not because you are hoping to make them jealous or sorry that they did not snatch you up), then it is fine to invite your ex-lovers. However, Ms. Behavior has found that it is best to limit your combined ex-lovers to no more than 35 percent of the total guest list. A more complicated formula is to divide the number of ex-lovers you have by the number of months it has been since you have slept with each of them and use the result of that equation to determine the number of ex-lovers to invite. Whatever you do, do not put them all at the same table. Midway through the reception, you will suddenly realize that they are all laughing, pointing, and imitating the noise you used to make in bed, which will make you very nervous.

Question: *Should we invite our relatives, even those who seem less than accepting of our deviant lifestyle?*

Ms. Behavior's answer: If you feel comfortable having them there, it is fine to invite them. If you think they might put any sort of damper on your enjoyment, forget it. Especially if they might be prone to asking when you are going to have a "real" wedding. If, however, they are very rich and very generous, you might consider inviting them anyway. Every time they bug you, just conjure up a mental image of the new Range Rover their money will be put toward.

Question: *If my lover is planning to wear a tux, do I have to wear a dress, by default?*

Ms. Behavior's answer: Ms. Behavior believes that regardless of your gender or what your lover is wearing, you should wear a dress only if you look really fierce in one.

Question: *My future husband and I have been fighting endlessly about what kind of flowers to have at our commitment ceremony. He wants all white freesias, and I want a huge, colorful assortment of all different types of exotic flowers. Is trouble on the horizon?*

Ms. Behavior's answer: Yes.

Question: *Isn't gay and lesbian marriage merely a way of embracing the heterosexual paradigm, which is based on ownership, control, and the subjugation of women?*

Ms. Behavior's answer: No. Marriage can be based on love and commitment without ownership. Your parents never should have sent you to that Seven Sisters school. Your mind has been warped by too many feminist studies classes.

Question: *When will you get married, Ms. Behavior?*

Ms. Behavior's answer: Ms. Behavior will get married when the woman of her dreams proclaims her love and devotion by revealing a freshly scabbed tattoo of Ms. Behavior's name on her left buttock during the celebration of the summer solstice, while serenading Ms. Behavior with her favorite Holly Near song and feeding her carob-coated rice cakes with her fingers. Only then 'til death do us part.

Part Seven

BREAKING UP
& OTHER
TRAGEDIES

Chapter Forty-Five

✦ ✦ ✦

THE ETIQUETTTE OF

BREAKING UP

*M*s. Behavior suspects that life is sometimes easier for pessimists, those sad-eyed, mopey individuals who have perfected the art of low expectations. For this reason, when Ms. Behavior meets a woman she likes, she begins to refer to her as her future ex-lover, even before they get involved. Why not take the sting out of the ending as early as possible? In her more cynical moments, Ms. Behavior believes that just as we begin to die as soon as we're born, we start to break up as soon as we begin a relationship. (From this point of view, every meal you eat together is another wrinkle in the life of your relationship, every movie you see together an age spot, every time you make love a metaphorical loss of hair.)

Breaking up is a sad and ugly business. It's no wonder so many couples stay together even after succumbing to lack of interest or Lesbian Bed Death (or Waltz of the One-Eyed Wanderer, the gay male equivalent). If you happen to have found some reasons to dislike your lover along the way, your transition into creating separate lives will be easier. If you have realized that you can't stand her friends, or that he is not nearly affectionate enough anyway, consider yourself lucky. Otherwise, prepare for a lot of crying, wailing, and keening; you cannot avoid the heartbreak that comes with ending a love relationship.

A little bit of tact goes a long way when it comes to discussing reasons for leaving. Kindness dictates sticking with a general form of the truth, like "We've evolved to a place of conflict [or deadness, or miscommunication, or whatever] that I don't think can be resolved, and I think we need to change the form of our relationship to a friendship." Do not say that you are leaving because you have not been attracted to your lover ever since he became a chocolate-chip-cookie-eating, non-gym-going blimp on wheels. Do not say that you are leaving because you worry that her parent's emotional and mental disorders might be genetic. And do not say, "I was never really attracted to you anyway. I would like to find someone with a smaller nose and bigger shoulders." If you are the one who is leaving, the least you can do is be gracious about it and not force your lover into a black hole of declining self-esteem.

Splitting up household possessions can be nasty. Ms. Behavior believes that it is better to let go of your Calphalon pots and your Irish linen tablecloths than it is to become petty over material goods. If you are being abandoned by your philandering lover, perhaps you can get your way a bit more (and keep the china settings you were given as a housewarming present), since your partner will probably feel guilty. If you are the one who is leaving, however, you should at least try to be magnanimous. You have more control and more self-esteem, for the moment, so do not take all of the Marilyn Monroe prints and all of the drag wigs. Remember that your partner will have an empty shell of a life for a while, without you. You can afford to be generous.

Going through the process of ending may arouse a desire to be mean so that you can detach from your sad feelings. But Ms. Behavior believes it is best to break up as gently as possible. Even if you are inspired to be kind for karmic reasons alone, it is a worthwhile endeavor. (Otherwise, in your next life you might be cruelly dumped by all your lovers, or, even worse, regardless of your current gender, you will be born as a Woman Who Loves Too Much.)

Being nice should not include trying to assuage your own guilt by using lines or explanations that are meant to be pleasant but will only make your lover feel worse. Do not, for example, use the most horrible breakup line ever, "It's not you, it's me." Or, dreadful variation, "You deserve better than me, and I just want to give you space to find the person who will make you happy." If you say one of these insulting things, which implies that your lover is a pathetic idiot, Ms. Behavior thinks it would be perfectly appropriate for the jilted ex to drive a long, rusty stake through your shriveled heart.

The best possible breakup circumstances are mutual, when you and your lover both conclude that your era as lovers is over and that it is time to move on. You maturely discuss the possibility (or, for lesbians, the inevitability) of being friends and accept that the romance is over. Unfortunately, you will rarely be so lucky. Most of the time at least one of you will have your tender chest ripped open and will be left a heaving, bleeding mass of flesh.

Basically, breaking up comes down to the torture of being the dumper or the agony of being the dumpee. It is Ms. Behavior's belief that being dumped is easier, because you get to cry, yell, and write bitter poetry. No one will criticize you if you leave stacks of dirty dishes in your sink for weeks, and you can dress in black clothing to achieve the forlorn widow effect. You don't have to wash your hair for days, and you can eat only Yodels and pizza pockets. Ms. Behavior would recommend making an appointment for an extra therapy session and then just sitting there and rocking without even speaking. Being dumped is a valuable opportunity for the expression of high drama.

When your lover discards you like so much trash, your friends will support you and tell you that your ex was never worthy of your devotion anyway and that you can call them any time of the day or night to cry and moan. They will sit on your couch hugging you, hand you tissues, and bring you frozen yogurt, which you will nibble at pitifully. You might even become thin for a while!

When you are the one who does the dirty dumping deed, your life is not nearly so grand. Not only do you have to deal with the guilt of leaving someone who still wants you and is now whimpering and living on Twinkies, you also get little or no support from your friends, because they assume that you are the strong one. Your mutual friends flock to support the underdog, which is not you. Be prepared for a lot of cold nights spent alone, watching *Lady Sings the Blues* and *Mildred Pierce.*

One of the really annoying aspects of breaking up is having to deal with other people's responses. Some of your acquaintances will look at you dolefully and say, "But you two were so *perfect* together. Oh, this is terrible. I am just so sad," and on and on and on. Try not to push them into traffic.

Other people will pretend that they don't notice. These are the same people who would not acknowledge that anything was different if you had the misfortune to lose an arm in a car wreck and began to show up at social events with only a stump. After a while you might want to poke them (with your good arm) and say, "*Hey.* Do you notice anything different??"

Then there are those who will ask you directly where your lover is. They will look concerned, and some actually are, but often the people who act most interested are just vulturous gossipmongers. To these people it is best to respond by saying that your lover has been missing for a while. Then ask them if they can come back to your apartment to help you move something into your car. Mention that it is a very heavy Hefty bag and ask them not to tell anyone.

Over time, you will grow less sad or bitter about your breakup. If you are a gay man, you may go on with your life fairly quickly and meet other men. Your emotional angst might be intense, but it is likely to be briefer than a lesbian's. A pair of pecs at work or at the gym will catch your eye, and you will soon be on your way to a happy form of forgetting.

If you are a lesbian, however, it is very likely (and practically required) that you and your ex will eventually be friends. One day your softball team will play hers and you will make up. Or you will run into her on the beach or at a fundraiser and she will make you laugh, and you will remember why you once liked her. Soon you will be having lunch together once a week and you will be close, supportive lesbian buddies.

Before you know it, your ex will invite you to a vegetarian potluck dinner, and you will realize, looking around the table, that you have become part of her large network of ex-lovers. You all bond by joking about your ex's silly quirks, which feels like a big relief of tension. One of the women at the table is likely to catch your attention, because she will be the funniest one in the room, or the one with the brightest eyes. You will remember the stories that your lover told you about her, about what a jealous person she was, or how good she was in bed, or how wonderful her cooking was. By the end of the evening you will realize that you have met your next future ex-lover, and you will find yourself grinning happily because you are a part of the big cosmic lesbian cycle of nature, and you are keeping your heritage alive.

Chapter Forty-Six

✦ ✦ ✦

ARE YOU A DRAMA
QUEEN OR DO YOU
JUST PLAY ONE
ON TV?

*M*s. Behavior loves Drama Queens, those histrionic homo-sexuals who were called Chicken Little even as far back as elementary school for their pessimism and who appreciate the suicidal songs that keep tissue manufacturers and Tylenol salesmen in business. Part of what Ms. Behavior appreciates about Drama Queens is that delicate balance they maintain between girlish hopefulness and tragic intuition, which allows them to dream innocently and be dev-astatingly crushed over and over again, only to emerge triumphantly hopeful once more, concealer barely covering their bruises.

Drama Queens give themselves fully to love, or even to the teensi-est potential of love, but only when they know, perhaps unconsciously, that there is absolutely no chance for a happy outcome. Seemingly unlucky in relationships, Drama Queens tend to get involved with straight men, married men, men who are leaving town, dying men,

men who will never love them enough, men who are hopelessly free of compassion, humor, or fashion sense, and men who are in love with someone else. Then, when their relationships predictably end, Drama Queens sob for months, swearing that they never saw it coming, and spend their evenings walking up and down the yellow painted line on the subway platform, hanging one foot mournfully over the edge, writing their own eulogies and the guest lists for their funerals.

Drama Queens claim to be suicidal but are too enamored of the tragedy of their lives ever to seriously consider offing themselves. They do, however, enjoy planning their own demise, which usually involves such Hollywood methods as putting their head in the gas oven or finding long pieces of sturdy but colorful ribbon from which to hang. The most enjoyable part of these suicidal fantasies consists of planning the fabulous outfits in which they will be found and preparing the graceful positioning of their long, attractive limbs. Sometimes Drama Queens have practice sessions, in which they don their death outfits, apply their beautiful but subtle makeup, and lie on the floor in their kitchen, quietly slipping into *faux* unconsciousness as imaginary gas fumes fill the room.

An inordinate appreciation for other people's tragedies, sometimes masked as great sympathy, is frequently a symptom of Drama Queenism. A preoccupation with a distant relative's decline into poor health or the need to recount incessantly the grisly details of a friend's torturous anal wart-removal procedure is a likely indication of this characteristic. If you ever need someone to sit by your bedside while you're recovering from a gallbladder operation, just call on a Drama Queen. She will be happy to clean your wound, change your bandages, and bring you tea, as long as you don't mind hearing about the evil man who dumped her just when she knew she was *really* in love, for the first time *ever.*

Do you wonder if you are a Drama Queen? Ms. Behavior's quiz will provide you with a definite answer.

1. Do you know every last detail of the deaths of the Drama Queen's supreme role models, Judy Garland, Billie Holiday, Marilyn Monroe, and Jayne Mansfield?

2. Can you lip-synch all the words to "The Way We Were"?

3. Do you find that sometimes you don't really mind having bad things happen to you, as long as you know that you will later get to talk about your suffering?

4. If you were watching a sad Bette Davis movie and the electricity went out, would you hook up a generator to your exercise bicycle and pedal your ass off to be able to watch the rest?

5. Do you tell people that Christina Crawford's childhood was better than yours?

6. Do you think any man you love is destined to make you want and need him desperately and then to leave you for a cute young stud with buns of steel and a low IQ?

7. Have you ever thrown yourself across your bed with an empty prescription bottle at your side, hoping someone will find you and think you have overdosed?

8. Do you think Baby Jane's sister did the right thing by not telling her secret until the end?

9. Do you suspect that pessimistic and melancholy people are ultimately happier than anyone else?

10. Do you still cling to the waning hope that the man of your dreams will emerge from the rubble of your life and offer you salvation in the form of undying passion?

11. Do you smoke more cigarettes than you really want, just so you cough a lot and it sounds like you have emphysema?

12. Do you own recordings of at least two of the following three

songs: "You Always Hurt the One You Love," "I Will Survive," and "One Less Bell to Answer"?

13. Are your favorite movies the ones in which the heroine dies, or becomes crippled or blind?

Scoring: Give yourself one point for every yes.

Nine to thirteen points: Congratulations! You are a full-fledged Drama Queen, and all the world is your stage. If Ms. Behavior ever gets hired as a casting director, she will keep you around at all times, because she understands and appreciates the rare and special beauty of your dramatic range.

Four to eight points: Your responses to things are fairly sensible, and your sense of dramatic reaction is within a normal range. You are perfectly capable of describing all the ways in which the world is unfair. You would probably do well to don a long robe occasionally and stand in front of your window wearing a turban and lip-synching a Puccini opera. Someday you should really let your hair down and scream at the top of your lungs.

Three or fewer points: You have no dramatic sensibility at all. You need to spend the next six months of your life watching movies like *Magnificent Obsession* and *An Affair to Remember* and reading books in which young love is extinguished by tragic endings. Ms. Behavior does not understand where you went wrong. She suspects that you might not even be gay, and suggests an immediate evaluation by a professional.

Chapter Forty-Seven

✦ ✦ ✦

EX-LOVERS ARE
FOREVER

*G*ay men know something lesbians do not know. They have this uncanny ability to let go of lovers they no longer want to be with. Like reptiles shedding a used-up skin, they emerge anew and just carry on with their lives. In fact, Ms. Behavior has witnessed male friends fail even to glance twice at ex-lovers who sit next to them on trains. What sort of behavior is this?

Ms. Behavior's friend Oogie tries to explain: "Gay men don't hang out with their ex-lovers because once the passion is gone, why bother? Who wants to be saddled with a dead romance when there are so many other luscious men to meet?"

Ms. Behavior is aware that some readers may not initially understand the benefit of being able to detach from a former lover; these are probably the same people who have never been consumed by the nauseous feeling that comes with having guiltily succumbed to an ex's sad-eyed manipulation for yet another night. Or the odd feeling that comes when you host a party and realize that all of the guests are people with whom you have showered.

Not all gay men, of course, fit the pattern of easy detachment.

Ms. Behavior's friend the Trouser Trout has remained friends with all of his ex-boyfriends, even the one he found frolicking naked in the living room with his entire college lacrosse team. He says he finds it easy to maintain friendships after breaking up because most of his love relationships have felt more like friendships anyway. (His lesbian therapist has a different explanation, something about the Trout's having stored rage in his spine, which "blocks the energy of his true loving feelings." She is trying to release this rage by tapping his neck with a feather.)

Unlike typical gay male couples, lesbians bond for life. If you're a woman choosing a lover, you might want to keep this fact in mind: Your sexual relationship may be of limited duration, but you will be stuck with that special ex-lover/friend bond forever and ever. This means that any lesbian whom you can't envision sitting at your dinner table during Thanksgiving in the year 2015 is not a suitable romantic partner.

The longer you remain a lesbian, the more your circle of ex-lovers becomes a roster of women who feel like aunts or cousins. As each holiday passes, you find more and more dykes cluttering your dining room, and one day you choke on your cranberry sauce, looking around the table and realizing that you have touched tongues with what feels like your entire extended family. Oh God! It's like sleeping with your Aunt Pearl (and your Aunt Esther, and your Aunt Minnie, and your Aunt . . .).

It's even worse for women who engage in team sports. Ms. Behavior's friend Odetta recently displayed a picture of her softball team and pointed out teammates who were currently or formerly coupled. It was so confusing to Ms. Behavior that Odetta had to draw a graph, a kind of lesbian family tree, which connected various bat-wielding women to each other with Magic Marker lines. Still, even with the geneagram, Ms. Behavior needed a calculator to understand the various permutations of these dykey dalliances fully.

Why is it that lesbian relationships are forever? Have you ever wondered why you haven't been able to shake any of your ex-lovers?

Ms. Behavior cannot offer a definitive answer, but she does, out of a desire to be responsive to your every need, have a few theories she is happy to offer:

1. Remaining friends with your lovers is part of your lesbian ancestry and permanently ingrained in sapphic cultural identity, in the same way that Jews gather together to fast and then gorge on Yom Kippur.

2. As the most highly evolved human species, lesbians are able to transcend the lowly societal notion that a romantic breakup separates one soul from another.

3. You have to remain friends with your lovers or your field hockey team would fall apart.

4. It's not your fault. The community is just so small that it only looks like you're surrounded by ex-lovers.

5. You are so lovable that once someone loves you, she will always love you.

6. There are only two lesbians on the planet anyway; the rest is done with mirrors.

Chapter Forty-Eight

✦　✦　✦

WHAT SHOULD YOU
DO IF YOUR EX
WANTS YOU BACK?

*I*n the initial sad weeks or months after your relationship ends, everything sucks. You cry until your eyes practically bleed, and feel miserably alone. Who needs a mattress? You sleep on the floor so that your physical discomfort matches your emotional pain. Holding hot little matchheads to your skin feels good for the same reason. Your supportive friends continue to take you to the movies every weekend and try to drag you to clubs, but you wonder if you're using up their goodwill by whining.

Then, for no good reason other than the passage of time, you start to feel a little better. You eat real food and start to wear normal clothing. You start shaving again (your face, your legs, or both) and washing your hair every day. Sometimes you take warm bubblebaths and listen to classical music. Lying back beneath the suds, you relax and realize that life on earth may not actually be hell. Soon you buy yourself cozy new flannel sheets and get up off the floor and move back into your bed, where you burn candles at night and try to

239

meditate. For the first time in years, it feels as if you might even be able to consider dating someone new.

But wait. Not so fast. Because just when you are beginning to feel a little bit human again and not quite so fragile about having been dumped on your head, something terrible happens. No matter how you try to brace yourself for this moment, it still devastates you. What is this horrible thing that happens? Your ex-lover calls and wants you back. AAARRRRGGGGGHHHHHH!

Ms. Behavior believes that you should have a plan of response. Perhaps it is because when she was growing up, her elementary school still had a bomb shelter and held drills during which she had to crouch on the floor in the dark with her head between her knees, pretending to anticipate a big blast. Canned vegetables lined the shelves, and she and her third-grade friends squatted and imagined what it might be like to be stuck down there for months in the blackness, eating Del Monte french-cut string beans. Would you not have to brush your teeth anymore, or take a shower? Where would you make your final doody? Ms. Behavior realizes that a person can never be normal after being raised to anticipate situations like that.

Therefore, Ms. Behavior is left with the feeling that you should always prepare for the worst. After any breakup, the first eighteen months are critical. Your grieving lover will most likely come sniffing around to try to win you back, so you should plan your response. Otherwise, your possessions will end up back in a U-Haul, and you will find yourself behind the wheel, driving toward your old address with a heavy heart. Do not allow this to happen. Your original breakup was bad enough. If you reconcile, you will be sentencing yourself to a round of bonus misery.

Before you allow yourself to respond to any seemingly remorseful pleas from your ex, try to get some perspective. Make a list of all the reasons that you broke up, especially focusing on all the characteristics that drove you crazy. Don't worry about being petty. Did he wear socks to bed? Did she always leave piles of greasy dishes in the sink, even when you cooked? Did he act jealous and weird around your friends, marching around in his silky boxer shorts when they came to visit? Did she bring her dusty Nancy Drew books to bed and read them when you wanted to tell her about your day? Did he sit there like a big lump with his hands in his pockets when the restaurant check came? Did she call you "chubby" all the time and give you noogies on your head when you wanted to make love?

If you find yourself remembering some of these things but then saying, "Yeah, but . . .," you are in trouble. Your own perspective cannot be trusted. Now you are probably thinking back to happier days, when the two of you were in love, which is always a deadly exercise. If you are honest with yourself, you will see that most of your joyous times together happened in the first few months of your relationship; after that, it was mostly a lesson in endurance.

Breaking up is so awful that most people don't do it until it is well overdue. Ending a relationship takes an unnatural feat of will, because it is contrary to the force of gravity. It is much easier to stay stuck than it is to make the decision to move on. So if you and your ex finally extracted yourselves from beneath a heap of angst in order to part, it was probably the right thing to do. The only exception might be if you are the sort of person who breaks up just because you cannot stand intimacy, in which case you shouldn't be getting back together anytime soon anyway, because you need to spend the next six or seven years talking about this in therapy. Just tell your therapist that you finally realize that you have a problem with intimacy. This will delight her, because she will realize that you are in it for the long haul.

If your therapist is good, she might gently help you to remember why you don't want to reunite with your ex. She might echo some of the reasons you gave for wanting to break up. Do not get mad when she reminds you about all the times you came in crying because your ex stood you up, embarrassed you at a party, or told you he never loved you anyway. Although hearing this from your therapist can be annoying, she is probably not doing it just to bug you. Go easy on her. Remember: She is not your mother (she just plays her during your sessions).

Whatever you do, do not get back together with your ex out of fear that no one else will want you. Eventually someone will. If you need reassurance, you need only to walk around the frozen food section of your local supermarket to see that all kinds of bizarre people have mates.

If your ex quietly tries to make a comeback, it should not be too difficult to brush her off. If, however, you repeatedly tell her to get lost and she is relentless in her supposed affections and keeps sending you flowers and showing up at your office, you will need to take a stronger stand. Ms. Behavior is a big fan of the brushoff letter, especially if your ex is the one who initiated the breakup. Here is a sample letter (which is one that Ms. Behavior wrote to an annoying ex, Maxine):

Dear Maxine:

Please stop sending letters and flowers to my office. I am allergic to flowers anyway, and those smelled bad. Please stop sending me photographs of your stuffed animals, referring to them as 'our kids.' Also, I do not appreciate receiving your lingerie in the mail. I never liked the black teddy anyway; it made you look pale. I am truly done with our tiring so-called relationship. I plan to be with someone energizing. Being with you has made me feel emotionally anemic. Please go away. Thank you.

Sincerely,
Your ex-lover, Ms. Behavior

You will notice that although this letter is not excessively mean, there is no room for misinterpretation. Ms. Behavior was clear in her intention not to allow Maxine back into her life, even to the extent of acknowledging that she was looking to find someone new and energizing. Maxine only persisted for two more weeks before she was snatched up by a big biker with a tattoo of Yosemite Sam on her neck. This helped to solidify Ms. Behavior's theory that you will not end up alone. Everyone can find love eventually.

If you are having trouble finding someone new, do not use that as an excuse to take your ex back. Ms. Behavior recommends that you instead do the politically correct thing, which is to recycle.

Ms. Behavior has four ex-lovers who are still floating around (including the one who is straight and married, which for some people presents a special sort of challenge). If you want the opportunity to meet them, she will be happy to create a Recycling Location for Ex-Lovers, and she will drag hers along to get the program started. There will be a smaller area at the same location for male ex-lovers, and bisexual ex-lovers can hover in the area between the two sections, hedging their bets.

Think of your ex as a pair of shoes that happen to give you blisters but that might fit someone else perfectly. It is not necessarily the footwear that is bad, it is just the way they affect *your* feet. Send Ms. Behavior a description of your ex-lover, and perhaps a photo. If you can convince your ex to participate, you can choose from the other available goods. Ms. Behavior thinks the ad campaign slogan for the Ex-Lover Recycling Center will be "One Girl's Trash Is Another Girl's Treasure."

Chapter Forty-Nine

✦ ✦ ✦

YOUR EX-LOVER "TURNS" STRAIGHT AND INVITES YOU TO HIS OR HER WEDDING

There is nothing Ms. Behavior could say that would prepare you for the day you open your mail and find an invitation to your ex-lover's wedding to a Member of the Opposite Sex (MOTOS). Even if you have imagined this moment, holding the invitation in your hands will make you act weird. You might shudder uncontrollably, or giggle, or perhaps even cry. If the invitation also serves as your first notification that your ex has left the fold, you will reread the names over and over to make sure you see what you think you see. You will run your fingers over the engraved letters as if you can read Braille. You will ask a friend to read the invitation aloud, slowly.

Sometimes Ms. Behavior offers advice about things that she has not personally experienced. She wishes the ex-lover-getting-married thing were one of them. She wishes she had not broken into a sweat

244

and begun hyperventilating when she received her invitation to Jessica's wedding. She wishes she had not laughed uproariously for hours and then gone to look in the mirror to make sure she was still a lesbian. She is still not sure why she framed the invitation and hung it over her bed. Perhaps it was a challenge for all who might dare to enter her bedroom: See if you can sleep with Ms. Behavior and not turn straight!

Once your ex-lover declares his or her heterosexuality in the form of a wedding invitation, Ms. Behavior can guarantee that your mind will replay endless sexual encounters with her. You will hear her sigh and call out your name, over and over again. But then her voice will say something else, and her breathing will grow intense. You will realize that now it is the other name on the invitation she is calling: "Oh, George! Oh, George!" Ms. Behavior extends her deepest sympathy.

You invite some old friends to dinner, the ones who knew you when you were together. You tell them that your ex is getting married to a MOTOS. They joke about it in an attempt to cheer you up, but you feel annoyed and tell them that they should be more supportive. When they offer their compassion, however, you feel irritated and tell them that they should stop being so damn empathetic and just lighten up. When your friends leave, you start laughing again. You wonder how people can just decide that they are not gay anymore. You take out a pad of paper and start to draw up a notification that you are resigning from the club, that you have suddenly "turned" straight, just to see if it looks equally silly when you do it. You e-mail this notification to three friends, just to see how they will react.

You call your ex, and her fiancé, George, answers the phone. You ask for your ex. Her tone is friendly but distant. You congratulate her profusely and tell her how delighted you are that she is getting married. She tells you she is happy that she has finally found real love. You choke. She asks if you are coming to the wedding. You tell her that you wouldn't miss it for anything. After you hang up, you eat half a gallon of rocky road.

As the big day approaches, you realize that you have nothing to wear. You drag a friend along to shop with you, because you don't trust your own judgment. After all, if you would make such a big error in love, how could you possibly choose an appropriate outfit?

Your friend disapproves of most of the clothing that appeals to you. He finally talks you out of wearing all black by telling you that you don't want to appear to be a grieving widow. You secretly do want to appear to be a grieving widow, even though you and your ex broke up three years ago. You agree to wear the outfit that your friend chooses, since his judgment is not impaired by confusion masked as uproarious laughter.

You do not feel well the morning of the wedding day. You think about not going. But curiosity gets the best of you, and you find yourself showering and dressing, despite your greenish appearance. You take someone beautiful to the wedding as your date. You hold her hand under the table and lightly brush her cheek with your fingers. Although you try to spend most of the evening gazing longingly into her eyes, none of the other guests seem to pay attention to the fact that you have a same-sex date.

The mother of the bride (your ex's mother) tries to snub you on the reception line. You greet her warmly. When she pretends not to know you, you start to remind her of all the weekends you spent at her house, and how she always wanted you to sleep in the guest room and was annoyed that you snuck into her daughter's room. She gives you the glare of death and assures you that you must be confused.

You introduce yourself to the bride's father as an old friend. He behaves nicely and asks how long ago you knew his daughter. You explain the time period and assure him that you know his daughter intimately. The bride's mother pushes you along, smiling her evil, plastic smile.

The groom is tall and artistic-looking, and somewhat feminine for a man. You smile to yourself, thinking that your ex's taste has not changed much. When he comes over to your table and introduces himself to you, you wonder if he knows who you are. His face reveals nothing, so you consider whether or not to tell him that he is marrying a recovering lesbian. He seems smug. You want to pinch him, but you realize that it is not the loving way to be, so you wish him well. (Your fingers are crossed.)

Your date begins to get annoyed with your obsessiveness. She asks you to calm down and stop acting like some kind of KGB agent. You can't seem to help yourself. Eventually, she gets disgusted and tells you that she wants to go. You cannot bring yourself to leave. This is human drama in the making, and you don't want to miss anything. Your date finishes her champagne and yours and then leaves without you.

You feel stupid sitting there by yourself with no one to talk to, but then the woman sitting next to you leans over and says something. It is hard for you to hear her, so she moves closer and whispers in your ear. "I'm straight, so what do I know, but I always thought Jessica was a lesbian," she says. You feign surprise, just to see if she'll keep talking.

"I heard she had a lesbian affair in college," she continues. "I knew her from high school and we once kissed when we were drunk."

You realize that this must be Martha, the woman for whom Jessica was a hunk of burning love through her entire freshman year of college. "I am pleased to meet you, Martha," you say.

"Ah. And you must be her hot flame from college," she says. "So the rumor is true."

You just smile evasively.

By the end of the wedding, you and Martha have talked extensively about the joy and angst of having loved Jessica. Martha tells you about their first kiss and you tell Martha about the first night you and Jessica made love. Martha recites a few lines from Jessica's love poems to her, and you pull some tattered missives out of your purse to show her. You and Martha have a weird bond that you can't quite identify. You notice that you are laughing a different kind of laugh now.

As the lights come up in the catering hall, you and Martha walk out together, talking and giggling as if you have known each other for a long time. Martha puts her arm through the crook of yours, touching you lightly. You wave to Jessica, a tired bride in a wrinkled white wedding dress standing by the door with her groom. As you walk by with Martha, you see something in her eye that looks like jealousy, and you know that the universe is perfect.

AUTHOR'S NOTE

Although the universe is perfect, Ms. Behavior realizes that there may be times that you feel it is spinning off its axis and rushing toward your head. During such times of distress, Ms. Behavior wants nothing more than to help make the world a safe and nurturing place for you.

If you need help or reassurance or have a burning question for Ms. Behavior, please write to her:

Ms. Behavior
c/o Houghton Mifflin Company
215 Park Avenue South
New York, NY 10003

Ms. Behavior will respond in future columns and books. Until then, she wishes you only love and light.